Tax Avoidance from Birth to Death

DOWNLOAD ZONE FOR BOOKS

Go to

http://books.indicator.co.uk

and enter your access code
VZZ443

for instant access to all the ready-to-use documents, tools, policies, etc.
that complement this publication.

We have made every effort to ensure that the information contained
in this book reflects the law as at June 1 2009.

No part of this publication may be reproduced or transmitted in any form or by any means
or stored in any retrieval system without permission.

ISBN 978-1-906892-07-4

First Edition - Fifth Print - E01P5

Introduction

Tax Avoidance from Birth to Death

Legitimate tax avoidance is what this book is all about. It shows how tax can be avoided at key stages throughout life - from birth to death and everything in between. The Taxman may not like it, but it's well established that you can manage your affairs to legitimately avoid tax. The fact that these tactics might advantage you and disadvantage the Taxman is irrelevant. So why wouldn't you want to pay less tax? Much of it is simply not knowing how to, or being nervous of the consequences. Tax Avoidance from Birth to Death explains, in easy-to-understand language, what simple measures you need to adopt to pay less tax. Often there's very little involved - an election here or a gift there - but the tax-saving consequences can be significant. And you can rest assured that the advice is 100% safe to apply - it's been field-tested by our experts with many years' experience of legitimately avoiding tax.

As you progress through life, circumstances will change. In analysing the main tax avoidance concepts which might be most appropriate as you get older, various stages have been identified along with the relevant planning points. You don't need to read the book chapter by chapter - simply dip in to the section that's relevant to your particular circumstances.

Martin Attis ACA
Chartered Accountant
Tax Expert

Table of contents

Chapter 1 - From birth

Chapter 2 - Whilst growing up

Chapter 3 - Single people

Chapter 4 - Couples

Chapter 5 - Property

Chapter 6 - Relationship breakdown

Chapter 7 - Maximising income

Chapter 8 - Providing for retirement

Chapter 9 - Retirement

Chapter 10 - Death

CHAPTER 1

From birth

1.1. INTRODUCTION

Did you know that from birth you are entitled to tax-free allowances? For taxation purposes children are treated as separate from their parents so there is considerable scope for routing income and gains through them, to avoid tax right from the start.

Obviously, little planning can be achieved by a child on their own, but this doesn't stop it being carried out by parents, grandparents and other relatives/family friends.

For example, children receive money gifts. If this money is held in a bank account or building society it can generate income. These gifts to the young from relatives would reduce their estates for Inheritance Tax (IHT) purposes. However, how should gifts from relatives be invested to reduce any potential income tax bill? Some income may even be taxed as yours (the parent's) if you are not careful.

Yes, there are tax-free payments that you can claim as a parent. However, you will need to know what they are and how to claim for them. They don't come to you automatically.

Thinking really long term, there are the Child Trust Fund and baby stakeholder pension schemes.

1.2. AVOIDING INCOME TAX ON INTEREST

Like adults, children each have an annual tax-free allowance, which is £6,475 for 2009/10. Interest from banks and building societies is usually paid after basic rate tax (20%) has been deducted. So your children could be paying tax on the interest they receive on their savings accounts, unnecessarily.

Tax avoidance

If your child's total income is less than their personal tax-free allowance, you can complete a Form R85 on their behalf (they can do this themselves if they are 16 or older) so that they will receive any interest without tax deducted. R85 forms are provided by their bank or building society.

TIP

National Savings investments pay interest without tax deducted, but there are other similar products available.

TIP

If tax has been deducted from interest on your child's account, you can reclaim this from the Taxman for up to the previous six tax years.

1.2.1. The £100 rule

Interest on savings and other income up to the value of the personal allowance is tax-free, but there's a catch. If the income, e.g. interest, dividends etc., derived from parental gifts exceeds £100 per annum, the Taxman's anti-avoidance rules mean that all such income is treated as the parents' and should be declared on their tax returns.

Example

Mr and Mrs Jones opened a savings account for their daughter Bridget when she was born and have been adding money to it each birthday. Last tax year the interest on the account was £195 gross, and so was exempt (the gifts were made jointly by Mr and Mrs Jones; up to £100 for each of them is exempt).

However, this year the interest is likely to exceed £200 and so the whole lot will be liable to tax. Once £100 is exceeded then the exemption is lost entirely, not just on the excess over £100.

Tax avoidance

If your children won't be able to use all of their tax-free allowance in 2009/10, transfer some of your savings into your child's bank account to benefit from tax-free interest. Keep the interest earned on the gift below £100 in the tax year. It will then not be taxed as your income.

Example

On £3,000 with interest rates at 1% this gives £30 of interest - so well within the £100 limit. Even if you gave them £6,000 (two years' worth of IHT-free allowances for making gifts) at current interest rates you won't exceed the annual £100 limit.

TIP

The £100 exemption applies for each parent and each child. If you have four children, you and your spouse between you could divert capital that would produce up to £800 (£100 each x four children) of tax-free interest in your children's names.

Exceptions to the rule

Only income arising from parental gifts is subject to the special anti-avoidance rules. Grandparents (and other relatives) have the same annual tax-free exemption for gifts as you do. But income resulting from the gifts they make to your child is not taxable as your income. So...

Tax avoidance

Gift £3,000 cash to your child's grandparents. It's within your annual IHT allowance so there will be no IHT to pay - ever. Get the grandparents to make a £3,000 gift to your child, their grandchild, out of the kindness of their hearts. It's within their annual allowance so there is no IHT for them to pay either. This way any income that is earned on it is not classed as yours and so not taxable at your top rate of tax. But as the child is a minor you still have control over the account.

TIP

Open a separate account for your children for gifts from others, e.g. grandparents; the interest on this will be tax-free provided your child's total income is within their personal tax allowance. If you want to draw money from one of your child's accounts, take it from the one into which parental gifts are made.

1.2.2. Would an ISA be nicer?

What if you put the money straight into an ISA in their name - it's tax-free and a simpler approach? Children currently can't take out ISAs and you can't take one out in their name (although over 16s are able to). So for this tax year it's back to the grandparents.

1.3. AVOIDING CAPITAL GAINS TAX (CGT)

Every individual has an annual CGT exemption, which, for 2009/10, is £10,100. If you make capital gains in excess of this, they are taxed at 18%. Children, even if younger than 18 years old are also entitled to an annual exemption. Can you make use of this to reduce your tax?

1.3.1. Property

Anti-avoidance rule

If you give an asset to your child, the Taxman will treat this as if you sold it to them at market value. This tax "anti-avoidance" rule can actually be used against him.

Example

You paid £90,000 for a property in 1990, and despite the recent fall in the market, it is now worth £190,000. You don't want to sell it now as you think the value will improve. But the more you sell it for, the more CGT you'll pay. Is there a way to avoid this?

If you have two children, you can give one of them a tenth share in the property now (in 2009/10 tax year), and the other a similar share after April 5 2010. That would be one gift in this tax year, and one in the next. The Taxman treats both gifts as sales at market value producing a capital gain of approximately £9,600 for each. As the gains fall into two tax years, 2009/10 and 20010/11, you can use your tax-free exemption for each year to cover both gains, so there will be no tax to pay.

Assume values do recover, and you sell the property in the tax year 2011/12. This will result in a capital gain for you and your children. You will each be entitled to a CGT exemption for that year, which can be used to reduce the amount chargeable to tax. Altogether, by using your children's CGT exemptions you have sheltered up to £38,000 of capital gain and saved tax of around £7,000.

Tip

If you transfer assets to your children, make sure you have evidence. Draw up a deed of gift and have it witnessed. If you are not sure how to do this, ask a solicitor. It shouldn't cost more than around £350 plus VAT. But the overall tax savings could far outweigh this.

1.3.2. Shares

If you are feeling generous and want to share your wealth with your children, then the occasion of a birthday might seem like an ideal time to do so. Gifts of quoted shares are not generally free of CGT if their market value exceeds the cost to the donor (purchaser). But isn't there any way you could avoid a CGT charge on making this particular gift?

Example

Mr G holds 500 shares in Made It plc, which are currently worth £30,000. Five years ago they cost him £2,000. If he gifts all these shares to his daughter and has them put in her name, then the Taxman uses the market value of the shares and says Mr G has made a gross gain of £28,000, even though nothing has been sold. Even after using his annual tax-free allowance, Mr G has a CGT bill of £3,312 (£28,000 - £9,600 x 18%). Gains, after deducting the annual CGT-free amount, being taxed at a flat rate of 18%.

Use a trust?

The classic advice in this type of situation is to have a discretionary trust set up for your son or daughter's benefit and transfer the shares into that trust. Your CGT bill for this will be £NIL. However, there are some equally classic disadvantages to this:

- although the donor pays no CGT, the tax on the gain is deferred (held over)
- until the shares are eventually sold by the donee (recipient), who then has to pay the tax
- the transfer of assets into a discretionary trust is a chargeable event and will attract Inheritance Tax (IHT) at the rate of 20% on the market value of the shares. And this initial IHT bill of £6,000 (£30,000 x 20%) could rise to £12,000 (i.e. 40%) if you die shortly after making the gift
- a specialist trusts lawyer might charge you a set-up fee of at least £1,000 and an annual fee (including the trust tax return) starting at £300. The rule of thumb should be that these annual running costs are no more than 1% of the fund's value.

TIP

Only use the trust route for large-scale gifts. This way the admin costs are a small proportion of the gift.

Tax avoidance

Instead of giving all the shares in one go, why not plan to give away sufficient shares each year to use up your annual CGT and IHT tax-free allowances? For CGT this is gains up to £10,100 and for IHT gifts up to £3,000.

IHT

If you didn't use the IHT allowance during the last tax year, you can carry it forward to this year giving you £6,000 to play with. So you could, in theory, plan to give away £6,000 worth of shares every two years - assuming you need your allowances for another transaction. If a gift is within your annual allowance for IHT, then it does not get added back to your estate if you die within seven years of making it - saving potential IHT on it too.

TIP

Either plan ahead to use the IHT and CGT annual exemptions together and eventually give away your entire shareholding tax-free or just give away fewer shares tax-free this year.

1.3.3. What about using CGT losses?

If you sell an asset for less than you paid for it, then you have a capital loss. If you make a loss in the same tax year as a capital gain, they are set against one another. If the losses are greater than the gains, then you can carry the excess loss forward and set it against gains in later years. Therefore, you might think that it's a good idea to transfer a loss-making asset to your children so that you can use it to reduce any capital gains you may have. But beware, there's a trap!

Anti-avoidance rules

Unfortunately, the Taxman thought of this wheeze first. His anti-avoidance rules say that any loss you make on giving an asset to your child can only be used against gains you make on gifts to the same child.

> TIP
>
> If there are any unused losses resulting from gifts to a child, these can be carried forward, without a time limit, and used against later gains for the same child.

Tax avoidance

Assets given to your children are treated as a sale at market value. Use this rule before April 6 2010 if you need to use up your annual CGT exemption for 2009/10. Alternatively, create losses to carry forward and use against future gains.

Download Zone

For a **Deed of Gift** document, visit **http://books.indicator.co.uk**. You'll find the access code on page 2 of this book.

1.4.   TAX-FREE PAYMENTS FOR PARENTS

1.4.1.   Child benefit

You can't apply for child benefit until you have registered your child's birth and have a birth certificate. Depending on where you live, there may be a long wait for an appointment to register your baby.

You should have a child benefit claim form in the "bounty pack" (which contains things like baby wipes, disinfectant and shampoo) that you will be given when your baby is born. Otherwise, you can download one from HMRC's website http://www.hmrc.gov.uk/childbenefit/claim-info.htm From January 2009 child benefit is paid at the rate of £20.00 a week for the first child and £13.20 a week for each child after that.

1.4.2.   Child tax credit (CTC)

If you've not claimed tax credit before, you'll have missed out on this peculiar form of tax-free state assistance.

So what's on offer? A family can only receive one family element of £545 and one additional baby of £545 regardless of the number of children. The baby addition is paid during the twelve months after birth, not the tax year. Both of these are payable in full where your income is not more than £50,000. For couples, the limit is based on your joint income. If your income is above this threshold, the family element is reduced by 6.67p for every £1 of income above this. This is approximately £1 for every £15 of income.

If you have children and earn less than £58,175 (£50,000 + £5,450/0.667) in the tax year or £66,341 in the first year of your child's life, you should be eligible (some believe you should fill in the form even if your income is higher, to get into the system). That's good news. The bad news is that you'll then enter the labyrinth that is the claims process.

In theory it should be a helpful benefit: CTC gets paid to the main carer - normally the mother. It doesn't matter whether you work or not, you're entitled to it and you can be a fairly well off household and still qualify for some help.

The problem is that the calculation of how much CTC you may receive is so complicated that many of the staff who deal with the claims don't seem to understand the rules.

If you do put in a claim, don't assume that whatever you are paid is yours to keep. Basically, the amount you receive is provisional, which means if your circumstances change, you'll probably have to pay some of it back. In some cases, couples have been told to pay back thousands of pounds.

There have been some improvements in the backlog of cases, but the problem has certainly not gone away. Time after time parents said they had to repay CTC when they had already queried the amount they were receiving and been told it was correct.

Tax avoidance

Apply for tax credits. However, keep on top of your claim; inform HMRC if your circumstances change and be prepared to be as tenacious as a terrier when you're following it up. Keep a record of what you've sent them, what you've said and what you've been told, in case there's a dispute further down the line.

1.5.   LONG TERM AVOIDANCE

1.5.1.   Child trust fund (CTF)

Once you start claiming child benefit, you'll automatically be issued with a CTF information pack, followed by a voucher for £250 from the government (£500 for families on low income). You've got a year to decide where you are going to invest the money, otherwise the government invests it for you. Lots of parents complained that they've found the information hard to understand and have felt baffled by the choices on offer.

The problem is that it is difficult to get advice about what to do with your CTF. Independent financial advisors don't want to know - because the amounts are so small (you can only save up to £1,200 a year) it's not really worth their while. The CTF website **(http://www.childtrustfund.gov.uk)** does talk through the options, but it really can't point you in the right direction.

Tip

It's tempting to ignore the CTF information that comes through your letterbox. Let's face it you'll have far more important things on your mind. But it's tax-free money for your child. If you don't choose a financial provider, your child won't lose out entirely, but you (or rather they), could miss out on a year's worth of tax-free interest and you won't have control over which company runs the CTF.

1.5.2.   Pension from birth

The Taxman is bending over backwards to put as few barriers as possible in the way of people providing their own pensions. So much so, that since April 6 2001 you can even start a pension for a child. Sounds a bit crazy doesn't it, a pension for a baby! But...

Your child would probably have to wait until they were 50 before they could get their hands on some of the money. Most pension ads tell you to start early and you can't get much earlier than the cradle. The reason for starting early is that over the relatively long investment period (say, 50 years) there is an even better chance of building up a sizeable, tax-free fund. So how does this benefit the next generation? If their pension is taken care of, this leaves them with more of their own income to spend or invest when they eventually start working for a living.

Taxman's contribution

For every £10 you put into a pension the Taxman will add another £2.50. Up to a maximum of £2,880 per year from you plus a top-up of £720 (£3,600 x 20%) from him.

For example, if you paid in the maximum amount between now and when the child reached 18, then this would provide the child (at aged 50) with a pension fund worth about £500,000 - assuming investment growth of 4% net of charges. Worth doing, but what else do you get out of it…?

A saving on IHT

You know that if your estate exceeds £325,000 in 2009/10 you pay IHT (currently at 40%) on the excess. With the value of property these days it is quite easy to exceed this threshold. So giving away some of your own estate or asking the child's grandparent to do the same makes sense.

For example, the grandparent could pay a pension contribution within their annual IHT exemption of £3,000. A single lump sum of £3,600 (again, they only put in £2,880) for a new born grandchild would provide the child at the age of 50 with a pension fund worth over £41,000 assuming a net investment return of 4% per year. But this is for one child only, so use...

Gifts out of normal expenditure are also exempt from IHT. Normal expenditure means that your lifestyle is unaffected by the payment you make, so if you can afford the contribution to the pension scheme, then this gift will be tax-free. If you can afford more than one premium, then you can benefit more than one grandchild.

Tax saving

Where a grandparent invests £240 monthly (£2,880 per year) for a grandchild, the Taxman will add £720 at the end of the year making £3,600 per annum going into the pot. Paying until the child is 18 takes £50,544 (18 x £2,808) out of your estate for IHT purposes. Similarly, parents will be able to contribute for their children. The general tax exemption for pension funds overrides the settlement legislation which currently blocks contributions made by parents to their minor children.

Although the individual cannot draw the pension until the age of 55, this may not matter. It does free up their own savings to be invested in more flexible ways.

Tax avoidance

In 2009/10 start a pension for the next generation. This means that you can both save on IHT and get the Taxman to top up your contribution. Grandparents can do this for each grandchild.

KEY POINTS

Children and income tax

1. A child is a taxable person quite separate from their parents. Each child is entitled to a personal allowance to be set against income received.

2. Parents have a responsibility in submitting repayment claims and the tax returns when the child receives taxable income. A repayment claim cannot be made more than six years after the end of the relevant tax year. It is necessary to produce documentary evidence, for example bank interest statements to enable a repayment to be made.

3. Interest on money you invest in your child's name is tax-free up to £100 for each child. Stay within the tax-free limit by keeping money you give your children in a separate account from other gifts they receive.

4. The £100 exemption applies for each parent and each child. If you have four children, you and your spouse between you could divert capital that would produce up to £800 (£100 each x four children) of tax-free interest in your children's names.

5. Income from gifts from grandparents and other family members is not deemed to be the parents' and is not taxed until the child's income exceeds their own personal allowance. Preferred investments would include Government fixed interest stock, bank or building society accounts, National Savings investments, unit trust savings schemes and offshore funds.

6. Give £3,000 to the child's grandparents for them to gift to your child. This takes the money out of the IHT system forever. Plus, neither you nor your child has to pay tax on any income earned from investing it.

CGT and children

1. Children, even if younger than 18 years old, are entitled to an annual CGT exemption, currently £10,100.

2. Assets given to your children are treated as a sale at market value. Use this rule before April 6 2010 to use up your own CGT annual exemption for 2009/10. Alternatively, create losses to carry forward and use against future gains.

3. The classic solution of using a trust merely defers the CGT bill and could give rise to an IHT bill. As an alternative suggest using CGT and IHT annual tax-free allowances to make an appropriately sized gift every two years.

Tax-free payments to parents

1. Since January 2009 tax-free child benefit is paid to parents at the rate of £20.00 a week for the first child and £13.20 a week for each child after that.

2. If you have children and earn less than £58,175 (£50,000 + £5,450/0.667) in the tax year or £66,341 in the first year of your child's life, you should be eligible (some believe you should fill in the form even if your income is higher, to get into the system).

Long term tax avoidance

1. Once you start claiming child benefit, you'll automatically be issued with a child trust fund (CTF) information pack, followed by a voucher for £250. Growth in the value of this fund will roll up tax-free.

2. If your child's pension plan is taken care of by contributions you start from birth, this will leave them with more of their own income to spend or invest when they eventually start working for a living. Plus, they do have a really long period in which to achieve significant tax-free growth.

CHAPTER 2

Whilst growing up

2.1.　INTRODUCTION

It is often said that if parents stopped to work out the cost of having a child before the event they'd never take the plunge. Thankfully few get out the spreadsheets, or if they do, they generally keep quiet about it. And once you have children, you have much better things to do with your time than add up costs, but over the years a number of banks and financial companies have attempted to do just that. The figures vary widely but they're generally pretty scary; add in the cost of private education and, frankly, you're into telephone number figures.

Not surprisingly you can't become a parent without making financial sacrifices, either by cutting back on what you spend, working longer hours than you want or staying in a job that you'd rather not do because the salary is good.

One thing is certain, the more information you have, the better placed you will be to make the right decisions. This chapter isn't designed to be a comprehensive guide to all that goes with parenthood, but will give you some valuable pointers on the tax avoidance opportunities of having a family.

Many families wish to educate their children privately and this will require substantial outlay in school fees. Is there any way your employer/company could help in a tax efficient way? Little planning can be achieved by a child on their own, but there is considerable scope for planning carried out by parents, grandparents and other relatives/family friends.

The young are generally treated as separate from their parents for taxation purposes, with each child entitled to their own tax-free allowances for both income and Capital Gains Tax (CGT) purposes. Therefore, there is considerable attraction in routing income and gains through children.

2.2.　CHILDCARE VOUCHERS

2.2.1.　£55 per week tax-free

Paying for childcare can use up a large proportion of your salary, so if your company can bear the cost, you might be better off. One tax efficient way for the company to take on this cost instead of you is to provide you with childcare vouchers.

Your employer can give you childcare vouchers or pay for childcare directly, worth up to £55 a week with no tax or NI charges. That's 52 weeks at £55 = £2,860, for the whole year. And the tax-free limit is per employee not per child.

Whilst growing up

TIP

Issue vouchers monthly not weekly. The monthly equivalent of tax and NI-free childcare vouchers for 2009/10 has been set at £243 which is more than an annualised £55 per week. (12 months x £243 = £2,916 is greater than £55 x 52 weeks = £2,860). If your spouse is also an employee of the company, then that's a combined total of £486 you can receive each month.

TIP

Remember to alter your contract of employment to include childcare vouchers before any new salary arrangements start to apply. To the Taxman this is then part of your remuneration package not just another way of getting cash out.

TIP

The scheme needs to be open to all your employees otherwise the tax and NI-free limit does not apply. However, not all employees may take childcare vouchers because of the effect on their own working tax credits position.

Let's say you want £5,000 of childcare vouchers and that the company has to pay 8% of their face value to the agency providing them. The total cost of the vouchers to your company is £5,400. The tax-free amount gets deducted from the face value of childcare vouchers you receive, i.e. only the excess is put on your P11D at the end of the tax year.

Table 1. Your tax position with £5,000 of childcare vouchers.

	£
Value of childcare vouchers	5,000.00
Taxable benefit of childcare vouchers (£5,000 - £2,860)	2,140.00
Income tax at 40% on £2,140	856.00
Employees' NI at 1% on £2,140	21.40
Total tax cost to you	877.40
Net increase for you (£5,000 - £877.40)	4,122.60

Table 2. Your company's tax position with £5,000 of childcare vouchers.

	£
Total cost of childcare vouchers	5,400.00
Employers' NI on taxable benefit (£5,000 - £2,860) at 12.8%	273.92
Gross cost of providing vouchers	5,673.92
Corporation Tax saved (£5,673.92 at, say, 21%)	1,191.52
Net cost to the company	4,482.40

Trap. The scheme needs to be open to all employees, otherwise the tax and NI-free limit does not apply. However, not all employees may take childcare vouchers because of the effect it has on their own working tax credits position, or they don't have eligible children (under 16 and living with them).

Impact on tax credits

If you receive just the child element of tax credits (maximum £545 for 2008/9), then the receipt of childcare vouchers will not affect your entitlement to this. However, lower paid employees on the full element could be worse off by taking childcare vouchers.

Tax avoidance

By paying monthly you can still extract up to £2,916 worth of childcare vouchers from your company on a tax and NI-free basis in 2009/10.

2.2.2.   A lesson for the children

Saturday morning ballet or karate lessons were probably not what the government had in mind when it introduced tax relief for childcare paid for by employers. However, as long as the teacher is an approved childcarer, any different activities (e.g. personal tuition) offered in the course of providing the childcare will still be covered by the tax exemption. How is this possible?

This can be used on your child's education as well as care, as long as certain conditions are met.

Condition 1

The childcare vouchers, or direct payment by the company, must be used for qualifying care (provided before September 1 following the child's 15th birthday). This is generally the beginning of school year eleven/end of year ten, the final year of compulsory schooling. So you can't use this tax break to pay for last minute GCSE or A-level tuition. Just when it might have been helpful!

Qualifying care can be any form of care or supervised activity that is not part of the child's compulsory education. So as long as the subject of your child's extra lessons is not covered in compulsory school hours, in their particular school, it can be paid for directly by your company or with childcare vouchers up to the tax-free limit.

Condition 2

The second condition for the childcare to be tax and NI-free, is that it must be provided by a registered or approved childcarer.

Most registered childminders are not also qualified to teach music, karate, Latin or whatever extra skill you want your child to learn. However, specialist private teachers can register with the Department for Education and Skills to become an approved childcarer, if they provide their services in England (different regulations apply in Scotland and Wales). To do this the teacher must have: **(1)** a basic childcare qualification; **(2)** hold a first aid certificate appropriate to children and; **(3)** have a clean enhanced criminal records check. All of which you'd probably look for in a private tutor anyway.

Where the extra-curricular activities are provided by a club, the specific instructors must be approved childcarers in their own right, as an organisation cannot obtain such approval.

Trap. If your company reimburses you for the tutor's fees, or pays a bill made out to you personally, the tax exemption does not apply.

TIP

Get your company to make arrangements directly with the private tutor for the lessons to be provided to your child and sign any contract required. The full cost of the lessons is then tax deductible for the company and the first £55 per week is tax and NI-free for you.

Tax avoidance

Once a specialist private teacher has registered with the Department for Education and Skills to become an approved childcarer, your company can contract with them to pay up to £55 a week for your child's lessons (in any subject).

2.3.   SCHOOL FEES

Fees for private day schools can range from £5,000 to £10,000 a year. A school charging £10,000 in fees actually requires £16,949 of your earned income, because after tax at 41% (40% income tax and 1% NI) this leaves £10,000 net to pay the school. Ten years of this sort of expense means that you'll pay £169,491 of your gross earned income per child over the course of their education.

2.3.1.   Benefit-in-kind?

If instead, your company pays the fees directly will you have to pay tax and NI on this? When the company picks up the bill for something you would normally pay for yourself, such as your child's school fees, you are likely to be taxed on that expense, but may escape an NI charge.

Tax avoidance

With a contract between you and the School, you are liable to pay their fees. And if the company pays them on your behalf, it is meeting your liability under that contract, so the fees are treated as a part of your salary. The company pays employers' NI on the fees and you pay tax and employees' NI.

The trick to the benefit-in-kind route is to get the school to agree that the company is liable to pay the fees in all circumstances. This means looking at more than just the basic contract with the school, as the taxpayer in a classic case found to their cost.

The company had agreed with the school to pay the fees of the director's sons in letters between the company and the school. Invoices for fees due were rendered to the company, which paid them. However, the parents signed the school entry forms that made them liable for one term's fees if they failed to give a full term's notice of withdrawing their sons from the school, and they also paid the deposit personally. The bursar of the school gave evidence to the effect that if legal action ever became necessary to recover unpaid fees, the parents rather than the company would be sued for the debt. So the company was meeting a liability of the parents and employers' and employees' NI was due on the total fees paid **(Ableway Ltd v IRC SpC 294)**.

If you get all the paperwork right so that the contract is genuinely between the school and the company, you will still be taxed on the fees paid as a benefit-in-kind. The company is paying the school fees because you are its employee, not as a charitable donation. This was shown in the case **Glyn v CIR (Hong Kong) 1990**. The company had agreed in the taxpayer's contract of employment to pay his child's boarding school fees while he worked in Hong Kong. The school fees were held to be part of the taxpayer's total remuneration package and were taxable as a benefit-in-kind.

You do not have to pay employees' NI on the benefit-in-kind which saves you 1% NI. If you earn £44,000 and the company pays school fees of £16,000 per year, you will save £160 if the contract is between the school and the company.

TIP

Make sure that the documentation for all your benefits-in-kind is watertight. If there are matters that are unclear, consider getting further letters of understanding in place before the tax year closes. Otherwise there might be more tax for you to pay later. Those saying that all you have to do is backdate the agreements as necessary are not right. The Taxman (and the law) will see it differently, i.e. as fraud.

Tax avoidance

Get the school to agree in writing that the company is liable to pay the fees in all circumstances. You will still be taxed on that expense, but as a benefit-in-kind you escape any employees' NI charge.

2.3.2. Grandparent schemes

Grandparents are the source of funds for many school fee schemes. Often, however, they do not have enough spare capital to simply set aside the large amounts required. But there is a way around this.

If a parent sets up a trust for the benefit of their own child, the income arising in the trust is taxed on the parent (while the child is under 18), but if another relation sets up the trust the parent is not taxed on the trust income or gains. The most likely candidates for this role are the child's grandparents. Cash rich grandparents can simply place a lump sum on trust so the income and capital combined is available to pay the school fees over the course of the child's education.

Because the money has been placed on trust for the child, it is treated as if it were the child's own income and not that of the grandparents (providing the grandparents have excluded themselves from benefiting from the trust). Therefore, the child's personal allowances and lower-rate bands, which currently add up to about £43,875 (£6,475 + £37,400) per annum, are available to shelter income from higher rate tax.

Trap. If you give the grandparents the money to fund the trust that pays the school fees, the money will be traced back to you by the Taxman.

TIP

Where your company is likely to generate enough cash in the future to pay the school fees, then: **Step 1.** Get the grandparent to use their own funds to subscribe for new shares in the company. These shares are issued in a different class from those held by you, so a separate rate of dividend can be paid without affecting the dividends paid to you. **Step 2.** The grandparents immediately gift the shares into a trust that will help pay the school fees. The company pays dividends to the trust.

If the grandparent pays full market value for the shares there will be no Capital Gains Tax due on the gift to the trust (as long as the gift is made within a short period of time). Investing in a small private company is regarded as intrinsically risky, with the result that the dividends can be high in relation to the amount invested and still be seen as entirely commercial.

At present the Taxman does not appear to be attacking situations even where the grandparent's payment for the shares is nominal in relation to the income arising, but in the fast changing world of tax avoidance there is no way of knowing how long this situation might continue.

The key is to make the arrangements completely commercial. This way the £169,491 illustrative cost mentioned above could be reduced to an effective £100,000, a saving of over £69,000 during the course of each child's education. Worth thinking about!

Tax avoidance

If your company is likely to generate enough profits, get the grandparent to subscribe for shares in your company, which they then gift into a trust. The dividends paid on these shares can be used to fund the school fees.

2.3.3. Buy-to-let scheme

In most cases children don't have sufficient income to use up their personal allowance. However, if they had income generating investments in their own name, these tax-free allowances would not be wasted. So why not plan ahead and have an investment (in the child's name) that generates income to meet future school fees, but which also utilises these tax-free allowances.

As a parent, if you provide your child with an investment, the Taxman will tax the income (if it exceeds £100) as if it belongs to you so there is no tax saving. However, if a grandparent (or other relative) provides an investment, the income will belong to the child for tax purposes.

Another way to use up a child's personal allowances is to transfer enough capital to them for a rental property to be purchased. Of course you wouldn't want your children to have control over the property so it could be held in a trust with you as a trustee. Normally this would be what is known as an accumulation and maintenance (A&M) trust which your solicitor can easily prepare an appropriate trust deed for.

Once the property is in the trust, the trustees can use the rent to pay school fees. Trustees are required to deduct income tax at 40% from the payments so they should pay 60% in school fees and 40% to the Taxman. You can then reclaim the 40% tax on your children's income up to £6,475 each (that's a repayment of £2,590 being £6,475 x 40%). Recycle this to pay further school fees each year.

Obviously, you need rich grandparents to fund the trust. If you haven't got these, then a more modest approach would be for grandparents to pay the school fees directly. These sums are exempt from IHT as regular payments out of income, or covered by annual IHT exemptions (£3,000 per person).

Tax avoidance

With a rental property in an A&M trust for your children, 60% of the rents can be used to pay their school fees. Although the other 40% goes to the Taxman, claim some of this tax back by using the children's own tax-free allowances.

2.3.4. Using a bare trust account

Minors cannot legally "give receipt", which means that for practical purposes children cannot set up their own bank accounts to receive and then manage the money from, say, their grandparents. Consequently, parents have to open the necessary accounts for the children. However, the intention is that this capital and any income it generates should belong to the children and not the parents.

These arrangements are likely to be categorised as bare trusts for tax purposes. Each child must have an unconditional entitlement to both the income and capital of the deposited funds from day one.

However, funds within a bare trust may be retained by the trustees until the children are old enough to give valid receipt (on attaining 18) or applied for their benefit whilst under the age of majority. As the children are unconditionally entitled to the funds there are no tax implications on making payments for their benefit, whether the initial deposit to set the accounts up, any income subsequently credited to them or further deposits made. The children are taxable on any interest arising. However, they have their annual tax-free personal allowance to offset against this.

Trap. The position is, however, wholly different if the funds were given to you first, and you have then chosen to pass them on to your children. In these circumstances, you become the "settlors" of the bare trusts under which the funds are held. As the settlement is by a parent on an unmarried child, any income from it in excess of £100 per annum is taxed on you (the settlor). **Note.** As trustees you have a right to be reimbursed for this tax from your children's funds.

The question is, can you withdraw money from your children's accounts and spend it on them, e.g. for private tutors, school fees or maintenance such as clothing, etc. without any income tax implications?

> **Tip**
>
> Set the accounts up as bare trusts. During the life of the bare trust, you would be able to use the funds (under your management) for maintenance and education in accordance with the discretionary powers available to you as trustee.

TIP

Open these bank accounts in your own name and designate each one with a child's initials to show that the funds are held in trust for them. And of course, the source of the funds needs to be the children's grandparents not you, unless you want to be taxed on any interest earned.

TIP

Have a bare trust deed drawn up and make sure there is a clause saying: *"The trustees may pay or apply the income of the trust fund to or for the education, maintenance or benefit of [the beneficiary] and shall hold the remaining income on trust for [the beneficiary] as an accretion to the trust fund absolutely."* This should then fix the tax treatment on these accounts.

Warning. Unfortunately, the expense of a childminder is seen as an expense of yours (the parents) not the child's. So technically, when they reach 18 you could find yourself sued by your own children for misuse of their funds.

Tax avoidance

Set accounts up under a bare trust. As trustee of this you can then withdraw and use the funds for the children's education, e.g. by employing private tutors. However, don't use the money for childminder fees.

2.4.   CHILD LABOUR

2.4.1.   Weekly wage

Have you ever stopped to think how much your children's pocket money costs you?

Example

The cost to you of pocket money for a 15-year-old: £12.50 x 52 weeks = £650, plus 13-year-old: £10 x 52 weeks £520. Total cash per year £1,170. To pay for this, if you're a higher rate taxpayer, you'll need to earn £1,983 gross, as you'll lose 40% in tax and 1% in NI, that's a total of £813 in deductions.

With two offspring aged, say 13 and 15, funding their teenage spending habits could be burning through nearly £2,000 per year of your gross income, and that's before you take into account their mobile phones and free taxi service! There is a way to make these handouts tax efficient and improve your child's "work skills" at the same time.

Instead of paying the weekly tenner out of your own pocket, get your company to pay them a wage. They will have to work for their money of course, but every Saturday morning spent in profitable employment at your company may teach them something about the business as well as clear those little jobs that are always left undone. For example: updating websites, filing, data-entry, cleaning the company vans/cars, sweeping-up, shelf-stacking or counting stock.

As long as the task is safe and doesn't require heavy lifting it's perfectly legal to employ children aged over twelve. The hours worked mustn't take up school time, and can't be before 7am or after 7pm. You (the prospective employer) may also need to ask your local authority about permits, even to employ your own child.

Just put the teenager on the company payroll as a regular employee. To do this properly you should help them to complete the Form P46 (new employee without a tax record), as they will be employed for more than one week. The company will get tax relief for the full amount of their wages, and you get to keep more of your own after-tax personal income.

They will have their own tax-free personal allowance of £6,475 (for 2009/10) to use, which should cover all their Saturday morning earnings leaving nothing to tax under PAYE. There will also be no NI to pay, as children aged under 16 do not have to pay it (employers don't pay NI for them either). For the over 16s if you pay them less than £110 a week in 2009/10, there is no NI to pay.

How much?

The National Minimum Wage (NMW) for those aged 16 to 17 is £3.53 per hour. You don't have to pay as much as that to someone younger than 16, but it's a good benchmark.

> **TIP**
>
> Although aged between twelve and 16 and too young to pay NI, you should ask the Taxman to issue an NI number so you can complete your end of year PAYE forms correctly. Until this is issued you can use a temporary number but that needs to be replaced before the tax year-end.

> **TIP**
>
> As a regular employee of the company, it can provide your offspring with benefits-in-kind, such as a mobile phone. The business must own the phone (or SIM card) and sign the contract with the mobile phone company, to make sure it's tax-free.

2.4.2. Make them a shareholder

From a legal point of view, it's possible for minor children (under 18) to receive a transfer of shares in a company owned by you and be a full member and shareholder of that company (although the company has the power to refuse to register the transfer).

However, if you as their parent transfer some shares to your son or daughter, any dividend paid on those shares whilst they are an unmarried minor is taxed as if it were yours. On the other hand, it is possible for another member of the family to make tax effective share transfer to a minor child. The good news is that these issues don't arise where adult children hold shares.

Adult children

Once a child reaches their 18th birthday (or marries) the dividend is taxed on them (i.e. the parental settlement rule ceases to bite). A gift of shares to provide dividend income after their 18th birthday therefore offers considerable advantages. It is possible to pay a dividend of up to, say, £43,875 (£37,400 + £6,475) in 2009/10 tax-free to an individual (with no other taxable income). This is because the (10%) dividend tax credit extinguishes the (low) tax liability on that level of income.

You may find this a less painful way of financing the increasing costs of your children's further education. The dividend income can, of course, be applied by the child for any purpose or simply saved.

CGT

Any capital gain arising on the deemed market value of the gifted shares can normally be held over or it may fall within your annual Capital Gains Tax exemption (currently £10,100).

Minor children

As a general rule shares transferred to children by other family members or friends (on their own volition) should not be vulnerable to attack by the Taxman under the parental settlement rules, particularly if the shares have been held for a lengthy period. This will enable the dividends paid on those shares to be treated as the child's own income (invariably with no further tax liability).

> **Tip**
>
> As a minor child cannot by law give a valid receipt, the dividend income will be received by the parents as bare trustees, which could be used to pay school fees.

In practice, a transfer of shares by a parent to a grandparent as part of an arrangement to transfer them on to a grandchild is particularly vulnerable to challenge. The Taxman is likely to be able to sustain the argument that the parent was the real settlor in such cases. Also any preordained series of transactions are caught, as are reciprocal arrangements with third parties.

Tax avoidance

You could place some shares in an A&M trust for the benefit of your children. Dividend income paid to such trusts is not caught by the parental settlement rules provided the income is accumulated within the trust. You would be taxed on any income paid from the trust for your children's benefit (subject to the £100 limit). Unfortunately, you can't get around this income trap by making capital instead of income payments from the trust.

2.4.3. Partnership status

You could just pay your son or daughter a wage of £110 a week for 2009/10 and book it down to the business. However, the Taxman could argue that no work was done for the business, during term time at least, and disallow the deduction in taxing your profits. No tax deduction, but you would still be stuck with PAYE and NI. However, if you are a sole trader there is another way to pay them out of the business.

Why not consider making a child (who is 18 or over) your business partner? If you do this, their share of the profits is taxed as "self-employed" earnings so there's no need to get involved with PAYE. NI is limited to (Class 2 NI) £2.40 per week (for 2009/10) plus 8% Class 4 NI on profits over £5,715. Overall, you can reduce your taxable income and use your child's annual personal allowance. Everyone wins except HMRC.

A partnership agreement

Every partnership should have a partnership agreement (see the Download Zone).

TIP

Get your new junior partner to introduce some capital to the partnership. Initially this can come from you as an outright gift - the annual IHT exemption level for this is up to £3,000.

TIP

You don't need to make the new partner a sole signatory to the bank account. Leave yourself able to sign cheques alone.

TIP

With careful wording, you can precisely define the junior profit share. Set a percentage share which is low.

Example

Bertie's shirt shop usually makes a profit of between £70,000 and £90,000 a year. Bertie brings his student son Clive into the business. In the partnership agreement, the basic profit share clause contains: "Clive shall be entitled to 5% of the profits."

If Bertie brings Clive into the partnership on a £5,000 profit share, he will save £2,000 (40% x £5,000) a year tax, £6,000 in total over, say, Clive's three-year college course. As long as Clive has no other earnings, he will pay no income tax and NI of only £124.80; total for three years, say, £374. The family is £5,626 (£6,000 - £374) better off.

And the Taxman's view? Provided all the procedures for taking on a partner are carried through, the Taxman would be on very weak ground in suggesting that no partnership existed. In most cases it will be accepted without comment. But don't overdo it. If several children were sequentially taken on as partners, the Taxman might suggest that the arrangement was a sham to save tax and that the partnership income should be taxed wholly on the parent. This argument can be refuted with the following:

- profit share(s), although greater than the wage which might have been paid to outside employees, is not excessive as the family member takes greater responsibility; and

- the family member had been taken on as a partner in the hope that their succession to the family business could be established.

Download Zone

For a free sample **Partnership Agreement**, visit **http://books.indicator.co.uk**. You'll find the access code on page 2 of this book.

Childcare vouchers

1. Your company can give you childcare vouchers worth up to £55 a week or pay for childcare directly with no NI charges. The monthly equivalent is £243 (based on 53 weeks or £2,916 for the whole year. And the tax-free limit is per employee, not per child. If your spouse is also an employee of the company, that's a combined total of £486 you can receive each month. If appropriate, consider salary sacrifice arrangements to avoid even more tax with childcare vouchers.

School fees

1. Get the school to agree in writing that the company is liable to pay the fees in all circumstances. You will still be taxed on that expense, but as a benefit-in-kind you escape any employees' NI charge.

2. If your company is likely to generate enough profits, get the grandparent to subscribe for shares in your company, which they then gift into a trust. The dividends paid on these shares can be used to fund the school fees.

3. With a rental property in an A&M trust for your children, 60% of the rent can be used to pay their school fees. Although the other 40% goes to the Taxman, claim some of this tax back by using the children's own tax-free allowances.

4. Set accounts up under a bare trust to hold the children's money. As trustee of these you can then withdraw and use the funds for the children's education, e.g. by employing private tutors. However, don't use the money for childminder fees.

Child labour

1. For their "Saturday job" put the teenager on your company payroll as a regular employee. This is more tax-efficient then paying them out of your already taxed income. They will have to work for their money of course!

2. You could just give your child a summer job and a wage for their university vacation. But making them your partner/shareholder and giving them a profit share/dividend means you can pay the same but save on tax and NI.

CHAPTER 3

Single people

3.1. INTRODUCTION

If you have embarked on a career with a definite aim for your life, there may be occasions when you could do things in a more tax efficient manner, without getting the whole thing out of proportion. It makes no sense to neglect taking a few simple steps which could reduce your tax burden. A judge made the famous remark that nobody is under any obligation to order their affairs so the Taxman can put his biggest shovel into that person's wealth.

If you have no capital, or very little, but without dependants you will have few outgoings. The main objective would be to channel earnings into a savings plan. This may not be a settled period and any such plans should be as flexible as possible. Thus cash ISAs, high(er) interest bank accounts and National Savings products may be attractive. Once a level of stability is reached then an investment or unit trust savings plan might be appropriate.

3.2. WORKING

As an employee you are taxed through the PAYE system, under which income tax and NI are deducted at source. There is very little you can do to reduce your taxable income by claiming expenses against it. The tax rules about the deductibility of employment expenses are just too strict. However, a wide range of perks (from company cars to private health insurance) exists which allow you to undertake some remuneration planning, particularly as some of these perks are tax and NI-free.

3.2.1. Pay

New employees are likely to be offered a base salary and a range of benefits on top. However, your employer might later offer you the option of swapping some of your salary for further benefits-in-kind. This salary sacrifice arrangement needs to done by the book, so as not to fall foul of existing tax law. In a nutshell, the tax avoidance success of your salary sacrifice depends on whether you are able to give the benefit up at anytime and get your salary back. If you can, then you will be taxed as if nothing happened with tax and NI due on the original salary figure.

3.2.2. Expenses

You'll want your company to meet the cost of all expenses which have a business connection or relationship, no matter how remote that connection might be. Although you can claim tax relief under the general rule for those expenses that are "wholly, exclusively and necessarily" incurred in the performance of your duties, this is notoriously restrictive terminology. From a tax avoidance point of view, it's generally sensible to arrange that the company meets all expenses (directly or by reimbursement) which would not have been incurred but for the existence of the duties of your job.

The most common expenses are:

- mileage claims
- cost of travel to workplaces
- subsistence costs
- overnight accommodation and associated expenses
- entertaining.

Mileage claims

If you use your own car on company business, you're entitled to claim a tax deduction of 40p per mile for the first 10,000 business miles you travel in the tax year and 25p per mile thereafter. Getting your company to actually pay for business mileage gets the full amount of the claim out of the company tax-free, i.e. there's no PAYE to operate on it and it gives the company a deduction against its own Corporation Tax (CT) bill. It doesn't matter what form the mileage allowance payment takes, just that it's paid to an employee for using his or her own vehicle for business travel. So you can be paid a lump sum in advance of the mileage actually being done.

Tax avoidance

If your company pays you less than the 40p per mile, you can claim the difference per mile back from the Taxman, either by putting this on your tax return or writing a letter to your tax office.

3.2.3. Benefits-in-kind

The rules for taxing benefits-in-kind depend on whether you (the employee) earns at the rate of (it's scaled down if you start later on in the tax year) at least £8,500 (including the value of any benefits you receive). If you exceed this threshold or are a director, you are taxed on the "cash equivalent" value of the benefits. Unless special rules apply, the cash equivalent is the cost to your employer of providing the benefit not its value to you, less any amounts made good by yourself, of course.

You'll probably want your company to provide you with as many benefits-in-kind as possible (provided your personal income tax liability is not so large that it would be cheaper for you to purchase the item in question yourself). There can be advantages in a whole host of goods and services being provided by your company. Yes, there will often be an income tax charge on the benefit, but this is often less than the real market value of having that benefit.

Example

A higher rate tax paying employee wants to purchase goods costing £900. They would need to use £1,500 of gross salary, whereas they would be charged income tax on £900 (tax = £360) if the company provided the item.

Care needs to be taken with this philosophy and a cautious approach would be for the company to concentrate on first buying those goods which are connected with its trade and which you would have had to purchase personally if the company did not do so. The most common are:

- mobile phones
- company cars
- laptops
- health/back-to-work cover
- training courses
- pension contributions.

3.3. COMPANY CARS

3.3.1. Choosing a company car

You are taxed on the so-called "cash equivalent" of the benefit of having a company car. The cash equivalent is calculated as a percentage of the car's list price for every year or part of a year in which you can use it. The percentage of the list price used depends on the official CO_2 emissions figure for the car, which is fixed at the time of manufacture (see the Download Zone).

We have referred to the list price of the car rather than its cost. This is deliberate because the cash equivalent for the car is calculated according to its list price, not what the company actually paid for it. The list price is the price that a single car would have been sold at in the UK on the day before it was first registered. This price does not include any discounts given by a dealer, but it should include the cost of any extras worth over £100 that are added at any time. The list price of cars can generally be checked on the manufacturer's website.

So the amount you are charged to tax for a company car being available to you depends chiefly on its CO_2 emissions rating. Your taxable benefit will therefore be less if: the emissions rating is low; the car was only available for part of the tax year; or you have made contributions towards private use. However, if your company pays for fuel use for private as well as business miles, then this perk comes with another taxable benefit. It's the same taxable percentage as for the car itself but applied to a fixed figure of £16,900 (see the Download Zone).

Tax avoidance

You do not pay NI on the cash equivalent value of the company car. Only the company has to pay NI on this benefit-in-kind. And if you do have a say in which make and model car you have, pay close attention to its emissions rating. If it's down to a choice of two, you might be better off choosing the greener (lower CO_2 emissions) vehicle and saving some income tax. Also, think very carefully before letting the company pay for any fuel used for private mileage. Remember that all those little extras add to the list price on which your taxable benefit will be calculated.

Tax returns

The company car is a benefit from your employment with the company so you should disclose this on the "Employment" pages of your tax return, if you have been asked by the Taxman to complete one, that is. The cash equivalent value of the company car must be included in the section headed "Benefits and Expenses". The figure to use will be shown on the annual Return of Expenses and Benefits (Form P11D) completed by the company for you each tax year. The company has to give you a copy of Form P11D or a list of the entries included on it by July 6 each year.

You can't avoid tax on the company car by leaving it off your tax return. This is because your employer should have separately notified the Taxman when your company car first became available to you during the tax year. The first you will know of this is when you are sent an amended notice of your tax code by the Taxman showing a reduction for your company car benefit.

Your tax code

You do not pay tax on the company car before it is made available to you. The tax due on the cash equivalent value of it should be deducted from your salary gradually through the PAYE system while you are using the car.

However, if you were provided with a company car late during the tax year, or the amount of cash equivalent value for the car included in your tax code was incorrect, there may be more tax to pay. If the additional tax due is more than £2,000 it must be paid by January 31. If it is less than £2,000, and you submitted your tax return in good time, the extra tax will be collected through the PAYE system in the following tax year.

TIP

Check your PAYE notice of coding to ensure that the cash equivalent value of your company car has been included. Otherwise you will have a nasty tax bill to pay, albeit much later on. You should also check that the amount shown is correct. It is not unknown for the Taxman to make an error.

3.3.2. Running your own car

When the company owns the car, tax law says that you must be taxed on the benefit of having it available for your own use, whether or not you actually use it privately at all. Even someone with almost 100% business use is affected. Whereas if you use your own car on company business you're entitled to claim a tax deduction of 40p per mile for the first 10,000 business miles you travel in the tax year and 25p per mile thereafter. So which approach avoids more tax?

Example

Let's say the car has a list price of £18,000 and taxable benefit percentage of 28%. You anticipate driving 10,000 business miles and 2,000 non-business miles a year, i.e. 83.33% business use. For the 2009/10 tax year, the taxable benefit of having this as the company car would be:

Table 1. Taxable benefit

		£
Car benefit	£18,000 x 28%	5,040.00
Fuel benefit	£14,400 x 28%	4,032.00
Total taxable benefit		9,072.00
If your tax rate is 20%, your tax bill is	£9,072 x 20%	1,814.40
If your tax rate is 40%, your tax bill is	£9,072 x 40%	3,628.80

Providing your own car is one way to avoid the company car benefit problem. Yes, the company can reimburse you for the business miles driven at 40p for the first 10,000 miles and 25p for the rest; however, you will have to pay all the running costs. In our example:

Table 2. Private running costs

		£
Variable running costs (per the AA)	12,000 miles x 27 p.p.m.	3,240.00
Fixed running costs		5,000.00
Total outlay		8,240.00
Less business mileage reimbursed	10,000 miles x 40 p.p.m.	4,000.00
Net cost of running the car		4,240.00

Although as a 40% taxpayer your tax bill looks high (in Table 1) you are actually saving £611.20 per year (£4,240 - £3,628.80) by having a company car. The result will be even better if you pay tax at 20% instead of 40%.

Not having a company car is beneficial if the company can cover your annual motoring costs by paying you a mileage rate for every business mile travelled in the car. However, what are the chances of you making a tax-free cash surplus?

Tax avoidance

You'll have to do the sums in detail (which need to be altered every time there is a fuel price change). With fuel currently at £1 a litre, the 40p per mile is no longer such a perk, especially if you do lots of business miles (well in excess of 10,000 miles) as the rate per mile drops to just 25p. You'd probably have to give up your company car to do this, so look carefully at the fixed and variable costs you'll have to pay out instead. Don't make the change unless you can generate a tax-free cash surplus.

3.4. FURTHERING YOUR EDUCATION

At this stage of your career you might be interested in job-related training.

More tax 1

First the bad news; if you pay for the course (and exam) fee yourself and claim a deduction for this cost on your tax return or in a letter to your tax office, HMRC will not normally allow your claim. If you have made such a claim in the past but didn't get a negative response, that doesn't mean the Taxman accepted your claim, it just indicates that your tax return or letter was not fully considered.

More tax 2

As an employee you can only claim a very restricted range of expenses as deductions from your taxable salary. Any training costs (including exam fees) must be incurred in the performance of your duties, rather than as preparation for those duties. This test is almost impossible to pass. The examination is likely to be taken as the conclusion to a course designed to prepare you to perform certain tasks to a higher standard, or to perform some slightly different duties, so it is not strictly tax deductible. However, there are a number ways in which you can achieve the desired tax deduction.

Less tax option 1

Your first option is to persuade your employer to pay for the training, including the exam. It is generally up to you to choose when to sit a membership exam, unless your employer has a policy on this. When you book the exam date you contract with the college to pay the fee, so that cost remains your responsibility. However, if your employer reimburses the exam cost to you on production of a valid expense claim, you will not be taxed on the amount paid.

Less tax option 2

If your current employer refuses to reimburse your costs, you could ask a future employer to do so. If the terms of your new contract require you to have passed the exam before taking up the post, the new employer can quite legally reimburse you even though you sat the exam before taking up the employment with them. As long as you are in your new post when you receive the reimbursement, the amount paid is tax-free in your hands.

Less tax option 3

A third way is to claim a deduction for the exam fee from any income you receive as a self-employed business person. Unfortunately, the training cost is only strictly deductible if the course updates your knowledge, rather than prepares you to perform a completely new specialisation or provides you with a new qualification.

Limited company advantage

If you conduct your business through your own limited company, there is much more scope for getting a tax deduction for training costs. There is no restriction according to the type of course followed. The company can either pay directly or it may reimburse you for the costs you have incurred. The company can set-off the training costs against its income as long as the course was relevant to the business.

Tax avoidance

The best way to get tax-free training is to get your current or future employer to contract for the course(s) with the provider, under the banner of job-related training.

3.5. SHARE SCHEMES

Many employers offer shares or share options as an incentive. The tax treatment is complex. Some share schemes are approved by HMRC; these use employee share ownership plans, savings-related share option schemes and company share option plans. Small companies wishing to offer share options to employees can also take advantage of the Enterprise Management Incentive Scheme.

Tax avoidance

The feature common to all is that the profits made by employees on the disposal of shares acquired under such schemes are subject to Capital Gains Tax (CGT) rather than income tax. Thus employees have the benefit of the CGT annual exemption of £10,100 p.a. (2009/10).

Unapproved

By contrast, shares and options issued under unapproved schemes are subject to income tax and, if the shares are tradeable or realisable in certain other ways, NI contributions. Income tax is deducted under PAYE, which could cause severe cash flow problems unless the shares are sold promptly. Under unapproved schemes, however, the employer can still (subject to anti-discrimination legislation) choose the employees who are to benefit.

3.6. BEING FLEXIBLE ABOUT LOCATION

3.6.1. Relocation expenses

If you currently live more than a reasonable commuting distance from your office and move to a new home which is within a reasonable daily travelling distance, your company can reimburse all of your costs if you supply it with receipts as evidence of your expenditure, (although only the first £8,000 of the moving expenses will be tax-free).

Tax avoidance

If you had to meet £8,000 of relocation costs out of taxed income you would need to receive gross pay of £13,559 (assuming 40% income tax and 1% NI: £8,000/59%). To provide you with £13,559 of additional salary your company must pay a further 12.8% in employers' NI, so the total payroll costs to cover the relocation expense could amount to £15,295 (£13,559 x 1.128).

The relocation costs must be reimbursed by the end of the tax year that follows your move. So, for example, if that's November 1 2009 you must claim your relocation expenses by April 5 2011.

3.6.2. Temporary workplaces

If you are employed, the normal rule about tax relief on travel expenses is that home-to-work travel (what we shall call ordinary commuting) is not allowable. However, this applies to travel between your home and your permanent workplace. A permanent workplace is one which the employee expects to attend regularly for: **(1)** more than 24 months; or **(2)** for the whole period they hold that particular employment.

Certain employees, in particular site-based employees, do not fit this pattern. This is most common for building site employees, and computer programmers or analysts, who frequently get sent to different locations for their work.

> **TIP**
>
> If you are in this position and are working at different sites for 24 months or fewer, then make sure you claim your travel expenses.

Trap. There is another twist to the claim, however, which concerns the word "expects". If you have an assignment which you expect to last less than two years, you can claim all your travel expenses. However, if you are then informed, say, 20 months into the assignment that it is to be extended, your expectation will now be that the assignment will last for more than 24 months, so you are not eligible to claim travel expenses any more.

Not all assignments fit neatly into this pattern however. Your job might entail going to a main office or factory most of the time, and spending a few days in another location. It is possible under the rules to have more than one permanent work-place. However, a workplace is not permanent if: **(1)** the assignment there does not last more than 24 months; or **(2)** it takes less than 40% of the employee's working time.

TIP

Therefore, if you are a borderline case, try to arrange with your employer that the assignment will be either 24 months or fewer, or less than 40% of your total working time.

You will have to be dependent on your employer for this scheme. It is possible that HMRC will challenge this, and any form of written evidence will help your case. So it's better to have the terms written into a contract. You then claim the expenses by filling in a box on the "Employment pages" of your self-assessment tax return.

What happens if your employer wants you to work in a completely different part of the country, which is too far to travel to from your home every day? Can you rent somewhere near the location of the contract and come home at weekends? How much of this travel cost can you claim?

Example

Eddie's company provides engineering consultancy services and is based in the north west of England. It's landed a lucrative contract with MegEng plc in the south east of England. The journey from his home to the southern workplace is 200 miles and the contract is for ten months. Eddie takes a short-term lease on a flat, which is ten miles from MegEng's site.

If this ten-month contract doesn't comprise the whole period of employment with his company, then the new location can be regarded as a temporary workplace. This is good news for Eddie because he can claim the cost of travelling from his home to the flat and from the flat to the site. Because Eddie runs his car privately he is entitled to claim 40p per mile for the first 10,000 business miles in the tax year and 25p per mile thereafter.

Paying the mileage gets the full amount of the claim out of the company tax-free (i.e. there's no PAYE to operate on it) and it gives the company a deduction against its own Corporation Tax (CT) bill. If you just make a claim on your tax return, the company doesn't get any benefit.

Example

In Eddie's case, this total mileage claim for a 45-week contract would be 4,500 miles from the flat to the site (20 miles per day) and 18,000 miles for the journey to the South East and back (400 miles per week). This gives a total claim of 10,000 miles @ 40p = £4,000 and 12,500 miles @ 25p = £3,125: Total £7,125. Assuming his company pays tax at 21% and Eddie pays tax at 20%; the saving is £1,496 (£7,125 x 21%) for the CT and £3,201 (£7,125 x 31/69) in income tax and employees' NI for an equivalent net salary instead of a mileage claim.

Accommodation

The cost of the mid-week accommodation is also claimable if you have settled the bill, as are any subsistence costs, i.e. meals away from your normal place of work. These have to be reasonable costs and it's best for your employer to get them covered by a dispensation from the Taxman so that they can leave them off the end of year returns, e.g. P11Ds.

Tax return

If your company can't get a dispensation to cover subsistence expenses, all is not lost. The employee (you) can make a claim on your personal tax return for the expenses paid by the company, i.e. the expenses go on Form P11D but you put a counter claim for necessary expenses on your personal tax return.

Tax avoidance

Always claim for travel to and from a temporary workplace. It doesn't matter if you break your journey by staying locally during the working week. Remember, you still have to be working for that company after the contract ends.

3.7. REDUNDANCY

It is widely believed that an employer can pay £30,000 to a dismissed or redundant employee and that this amount will automatically be tax-free in their hands. As ever, the truth is more complicated.

Firstly, any payment that is a reward for services is fully chargeable to tax under the general charging provisions of employment income. The £30,000 only applies to payments (and other benefits) received in connection with the termination of employment if the payments are not taxable under any other provisions.

Where a payment in lieu of notice is made, it is necessary to consider the exact nature of the payment and what it represents in order to determine the tax position. Where there is a contractual entitlement and the payment represents salary foregone, the payment will be taxable. However, if there is no contractual entitlement, the £30,000 exemption comes into play.

Tax avoidance

The Taxman often takes an interest in the documentation surrounding payments for which the £30,000 exemption is claimed. It is essential that such documentation is kept to a minimum and is watertight. It is all too easy for employers to insert phrases such as "in consideration of many years' service which you have given the company" and thus to give you (the departing employee) a £12,000 tax bill (£30,000 x 40%)!

3.8. TAX-EFFICIENT SAVINGS

Some investments have built-in tax advantages: the government, usually for policy reasons, has provided an exemption from one or more of the taxes. Other investments are attractive because they fall within a category of asset which is favoured by the tax code. This section deals with both types of investment. It does not give investment advice.

To use this book as a means of choosing an investment would be wrong. Every investment produces return and every investment has a cost. Investment efficiency is to look at the return on the sum expended, after deductions of all costs. Taxation is one such cost for the individual investor. However, here are a couple of lists that should help you seek out the right specialist advice for you to be able to avoid tax on your investments.

List 1

Obviously, what is a tax efficient investment depends on your particular circumstances:

- an exemption from CGT has no relevance if you can confidently expect to have the full annual exempt amount unused each year

- income tax relief is no good to the non-tax payer, yet thousands of non-taxpayers hold exempt National Savings products

- every so-called tax efficient investment must be judged against other action available to you

- it may well be for you that paying off a mortgage or other loan (either in whole or in part), on which there is no tax relief, produces a higher effective return than an investment in an ISA.

List 2

The following may, depending on your circumstances, provide tax advantages if you are planning to invest:

- an approved pension scheme, whether an employer scheme or a personal pension plan

- investment in a private house to provide a tax-free gain on sale

- subscription by employees for shares under Enterprise Management Incentives

- unquoted shares providing 100% Inheritance Tax (IHT) business property relief (BPR)

- investment in your own business to provide 100% IHT BPR

- purchase of government stock or qualifying corporate bonds, providing the possibility of a capital gain that is exempt from CGT at sale

- putting funds into a company which you control where the company seeks tax relief under the corporate venturing scheme.

3.9.   PENSION CONTRIBUTIONS

You are allowed to claim relief against your income in respect of premiums you pay towards retirement schemes. However, in order to qualify for the tax relief, the retirement scheme has to be recognised by HMRC, and the rules of the scheme have to comply with HMRC requirements. These schemes are known as personal pension schemes. The main purpose of these schemes must be the provision for an individual of a retirement annuity in old age. The most obvious restriction therefore is taking benefits.

The main advantage of these schemes is that tax relief is given on premiums paid and this is available at your highest rate of tax. When you take benefits from your pension fund, a certain amount (up to 25% of the fund in the case of personal pension schemes) may be taken tax-free.

Generally, benefits may not be taken before the age of 55 for personal pensions schemes and 60 for retirement annuity schemes.

Tax avoidance

The relief is given at your highest rate of tax. The best time for making pension contributions is when you are paying the highest rate of tax. For example, abnormally high earnings because of an unexpected bonus in 2009/10, pushes your income tax rate up to 40%. Paying premiums in the same tax year allows you to claim another 20% (40% highest rate - 20% basic rate of income tax) of it back from the Taxman.

> **TIP**
>
> This principle could also be used when the basic rate of tax is reduced. For example, in 2007/8 the basic rate of tax was 22% but was reduced to 20% for 2008/9. The effect is not as great as the decrease from the higher rate of tax to basic rate, of course, but it can contribute to saving tax.

3.9.1. How much should you put into a pension scheme?

Everything depends on your circumstances. For instance, your age will play a large part. The nearer you get to retirement, the greater your concern that you are adequately provided for. If you are employed, obviously an employer's contribution will be much more valuable, whatever your age. On the whole, the best advice is to pay as much as you can afford.

KEY POINTS

Expenses

1. As an employee you are taxed through the PAYE system, under which income tax and NI are deducted at source. There is very little you can do to reduce your taxable income by claiming expenses against it. The tax rules about the deductibility of employment expenses are just too strict.

2. From a tax avoidance point of view, it's generally sensible to arrange that the company meets all expenses (directly or by reimbursement) which would not have been incurred but for the existence of the duties of your job.

3. If your company pays you less than the 40p per mile (etc.) you can claim the difference per mile back from the Taxman, either by putting this on your tax return or writing a letter to your tax office.

Benefits-in-kind

1. A wide range of perks (from company cars to private health insurance) exists which allow you to undertake some remuneration planning. Particularly as some of these perks are tax and NI-free.

2. New employees are likely to be offered a base salary and a range of benefits on top. However, your employer might later offer you the option of swapping some of your salary for further benefits-in-kind. This salary sacrifice arrangement needs to done by the book, so as not to fall foul of existing tax case law.

3. Your company should concentrate on first buying those goods which are connected with its trade and which you would have had to purchase personally if the company did not do so. The company does not need to enter into the contract for these benefits to be supplied.

4. The tax savings with benefits-in-kind is that generally you do not pay NI on the cash equivalent value of them. And that this sale for tax purposes is usually less than market value.

Company cars

1. When the company provides you with a car, all the hassle of car ownership is removed. You don't have to worry about servicing, the cost of repairs or insurance. The company also takes on the burden of a loan or lease to acquire the car, and will supply a replacement when you need one.

2. You do not have to pay NI on the cash equivalent value of the company car, although you do pay income tax on that amount. However, the value of the cash equivalent, which is the amount you pay tax on, may be greater than the cost of providing the car. It just depends on the CO_2 emissions of the car chosen.

3. The cash equivalent value of free fuel provided for private use in a company car is very high. It will not be tax efficient to have free fuel provided by the company unless you drive a higher than average number of non-business-related miles during the year. Instead, get the company to pay you the tax-free fuel only mileage rate for using the company car for business-related journeys.

Training

1. If you pay the training (and exam) fees yourself and claim a deduction for this cost on your tax return or in a letter to your tax office, HMRC will not normally allow your claim.

2. The best way to get tax-free training is to get your current or future employer to contract for the course with the provider, under the banner of job-related training.

Share schemes

1. Many employers offer shares or share options as an incentive. The tax treatment is complex. The feature common to the schemes approved by HMRC is that the profits made by employees on the disposal of shares are subject to Capital Gains Tax (CGT) rather than income tax. Thus employees have the benefit of the CGT annual exemption of £10,100 p.a. (2009/10).

Different workplaces

1. If you currently live more than a reasonable commuting distance from your offices and move to a new home which is within a reasonable daily travelling distance, your company can reimburse all of your costs if you supply it with receipts as evidence.

2. If you are employed, the normal rule about tax relief on travel expenses is that home-to-work travel (what we shall call ordinary commuting) is not allowable. However, this applies to travel between your home and your permanent workplace.

3. You can claim for travel to and from a temporary workplace (for fewer than 24 months). It doesn't matter if you break your journey by staying locally during the working week. Remember, you still have to be working for that company after the contract ends.

Redundancy/termination

1. The Taxman often takes an interest in the documentation surrounding payments for which the £30,000 exemption is claimed. It is essential that such documentation is kept to a minimum and is watertight.

Tax efficient savings

1. Every investment produces return and every investment has a cost. Investment efficiency is to look at the return on the sum expended, after deductions of all costs. Taxation is one such cost for the individual investor.

2. Some investments have built-in tax advantages: the government, usually for policy reasons, has provided an exemption from one or more of the taxes. Other investments are attractive because they fall within a category of asset which is favoured by the tax code.

Pension contributions

1. You are allowed to claim relief against your income in respect of premiums you pay towards retirement schemes. However, in order to qualify for the tax relief, the retirement scheme has to be recognised by HMRC, and the rules of the scheme have to comply with HMRC requirements.

2. Your contributions grow tax-free within your pension fund until you take benefits from the scheme. When you do take benefits from your pension fund, a certain amount (up to 25% of the fund in the case of personal pension schemes) may be taken tax-free.

3. The relief is given at your highest rate of tax. The best time for making a pension contribution is when you are paying the highest rate of tax.

CHAPTER 4

Couples

4.1. INTRODUCTION

If you are married, in a civil partnership or have recently announced your nuptials, or even just setting up home together, this chapter sets out some tax advantages and disadvantages you may need to consider.

Some couples find that one partner pays a higher rate of tax on their income or capital gains while the other does not have enough income to even use up their personal allowance and basic rate tax band. There are several ways of transferring income and gains between partners to take advantage of these otherwise unused allowances and bands.

Unless otherwise stated, these strategies are also suitable for individuals living together who are not married or in registered civil partnerships.

Get married to save on tax? If you take a long hard look at what you get by way of tax rights from being married, most of them don't apply until the point of relationship breakdown or death. It's probably not the most reassuring thought if you're contemplating getting hitched, but if we are talking cash, there are only limited tax benefits to being Mr & Mrs as opposed to Mr & Ms. However, these benefits can make a significant difference to any couple's tax bill, which is one of the reasons why the creation of civil partnerships was seen as so important.

So what are these key benefits and how can you take advantage of them? If you are married or in a civil partnership, you can give anything you want to your spouse or civil partner and not pay Capital Gains Tax (CGT), no matter how valuable it is. Also, when you get married you don't have to say "I do" to Inheritance Tax (IHT) too.

4.2. INCOME SPLITTING

Tax avoidance

Some married couples and registered civil partners find that one partner pays a higher rate of tax on their income or capital gains while the other does not have enough income to even use up their personal allowance (£6,475 for 2009/10) and basic rate tax band (a further £37,400 each in 2009/10). There are several ways of transferring income between partners to take advantage of these otherwise unused allowances and bands.

4.2.1. As a sole trader

Tax avoidance

A high income partner in a business could pay their low income partner a salary from that business. A salary of up to £110 per week is both tax and NI-free for 2009/10. However, PAYE records would still need to be kept of this employment.

A salary of between £95 and £110 per week will allow an individual to qualify for state benefits, such as the retirement pension, without any NI payment being needed. In particular, the individual will accrue benefits under the Second State Pension (S2P) as if the salary were £13,500. The remuneration must be reasonable in relation to the work done and it must actually be paid to the spouse.

As well as salary, a payment could be made as an employer's contribution to a partner's personal pension plan. The partner will not be taxed on this benefit nor will NI be payable on it.

Like salary, the pension payments will be deductible from business profits provided the salary and the pension payment combined do not exceed a reasonable rate of remuneration for the work carried out. Excessive pension contributions for a partner or relative may not be deductible on the grounds that they are not wholly and exclusively for the purpose of the trade.

4.2.2.   In partnership

Tax avoidance

Profits could be shared by operating the business as a partnership. Both individuals need to be involved as business partners and a written partnership agreement drawn up. Operating as a business partnership will not reduce tax if the business consists of supplying personal services in a form that is caught by the IR35 anti-avoidance legislation.

4.2.3.   Using a limited company

Tax avoidance

Your spouse/partner can receive dividend income if they own some shares in your company. This may provide a highly tax-efficient mechanism for extracting income where the spouse has no other taxable income. It is possible to pay a dividend of up to (say) £43,875 (£6,475 tax-free allowance plus £37,400 being the 20% basic rate band) to a non-working spouse without attracting any tax liability in the tax year ended April 5 2010.

Payment of dividends to your spouse can be achieved by: **(1)** the creation of a new class of shares; or **(2)** by you transferring some of your existing shareholding to them. Depending on the facts the Taxman may contend that such arrangements constitute a settlement. This would negate the tax advantage as the dividends would then be taxed as your income at your highest rate of tax. Similar issues may also arise with dividends paid to a civil partner on shares made available by the other partner.

Arctic Systems case

Tax considerations involved in securing a tax effective dividend for the spouse have been complicated by the Taxman's publicised views and challenges in this area. Notably the Arctic Systems case (more formally known as **Jones v Garnett**). However, this case does show that there are considerable limitations on his ability to apply the settlements legislation to shares provided to spouses of owner-managed companies.

A company was formed (Arctic Systems Ltd) which enabled Mr Jones to obtain work. His wife performed company secretarial duties for the company. She had no other involvement in the business, apart from purchasing the only other share. Over the years the company paid dividends on the shares of both Mr and Mrs Jones.

So, instead of all the dividends going to Mr Jones as the sole shareholder with him paying 40% tax on a good chunk, he was able to shift some of the dividend income to his wife by having her as the other shareholder. The tax saving comes about because (as a basic rate taxpayer) Mrs Jones didn't have any tax to pay on her share of the dividend whereas if it had gone to Mr Jones, it would have been taxed at higher rates.

If you did this in 2009/10, how much tax would you save?

Example

Tax saving on shifting income in 2009/10

	TAX BILL AS BASIC RATE TAXPAYER (£)	TAX BILL AS HIGHER RATE TAXPAYER (£)
First £6,475 0%/40%	-	2,590
Next £37,400 at 20%/40%	7,480	14,960
Total tax	7,480	17,550

Potential tax saving of £10,070 (£17,550 - £7,480) by shifting the maximum amount of income to your spouse/partner.

TIP

Get shifting your income, either by gifting shares to your spouse so they have a direct diversion of income via dividends, or by transferring other income-bearing assets to them. By utilising another person's tax-free personal allowance for 2009/10 (£6,475) and basic rate band (up to £34,700) you could save up to £10,000 in tax. So well worth looking at.

You might have to unravel this "arrangement" for the tax year starting on April 6 2010 (2010/11). However, you'll only need to do this if, and as things stand at the moment that's a big if, the Taxman manages to get any sort of workable form of anti-income splitting legislation off the ground and past all the MPs who indulge in income splitting themselves.

Tax avoidance

You can still legitimately shift income from one spouse to another in order to gain a tax advantage. But how much can you actually save by doing this? By utilising another person's tax-free personal allowance for 2009/10 and basic rate band you could save up to £10,000 in tax. So get shifting!

Associated companies trap

Companies controlled by individuals who are married are automatically associated for Corporation Tax (CT) purposes, even if there is no commercial link between the businesses. So from the beginning of the accounting period in which the marriage falls, the companies controlled by both parties will gain an associated company and the CT bands will be reduced. This can lead to increased CT liabilities, as some profits now fall to be taxed at the marginal or higher rate of CT.

Tax avoidance

A solution may be to merge the businesses into one company, however, this could create income splitting problems but only from 2010/11 onwards at the earliest. Another solution may be to dissolve one company and run the business as either a sole trader or Limited Liability Partnership (LLP).

4.2.4.   Splitting investment income

Investment income could be equalised between partners by switching the ownership of the asset that produces it. For example, shares could be transferred before a dividend is paid. For this to be effective, the asset must be transferred absolutely and unconditionally.

- in most cases, transferring ownership of assets would generally have its main effect on the income of future years

- transferring assets where the couple are not married or in civil partnership can result in a CGT liability and a potential future Inheritance Tax (IHT) liability

- transfers of assets between partners who are married or are civil partners are free of CGT and could save on CGT when assets are sold, if one partner has an unused annual exemption or capital losses

- savings could be held in joint names. Normally each individual is taxable on half the income. This provides scope for transferring income producing assets without losing complete control.

If you have a joint savings account can you just split the interest between you as you like? Will just putting the most tax effective split of that interest on your respective tax returns get you into trouble with the Taxman?

Example

Mr Saver - a higher rate taxpayer - has a joint bank account with his wife Mrs Saver (who is also a higher rate taxpayer) that yields annual interest of about £25,000 net. In 2007/8, he included all of the interest on his own tax return and the additional tax of £6,250 was paid by the due date.

Subsequently, HMRC opened an aspect enquiry into Mrs Saver's return, querying her share of the interest on this account. As no tax had actually been lost to HMRC, Mrs Saver replied that it was all on her spouse's return, but she offered to make sure that future years were correct.

Interest

However, the Taxman assessed Mrs Saver on her share and Mr Saver received a repayment. But the overpayment interest was less than the late payment interest.

Surcharge

It got worse. Mrs Saver will have effectively paid her income tax late, so she has laid herself open to a late payment surcharge. The penalty could be up to 100% of the tax payable on the interest. Although this only kicks in if the change to the tax returns is not within six months of the normal due date, i.e. January 31.

Mr Saver was taking an understandable and simple approach, but the treatment was incorrect. The **Taxes Act 1988** provides that jointly-held property for a married couple has to be split on a 50:50 basis. One solution is for a Form 17 to be submitted to the Taxman before interest arises on the account. In Mr Saver's case, provided the source of the money is from the husband, all of the interest could then go to him.

In practice, Form 17 will not be accepted for bank accounts because joint account holders are treated as owning all of the funds in the account (and they do not hold shares in an account).

Tax avoidance

Change your investments from "joint beneficial ownership" to some other basis by way of a deed. Attach this to the Form 17 as evidence to suggest the interest split.

Previously, inspectors might not have bothered to adjust the figures if both spouses were 40% taxpayers, but in those cases the interest received might only be about

£100. But with the ever increasing emphasis on meeting collection targets, the Taxman is now likely to pursue these small amounts. Many couples view their financial affairs in the same way as Mr Saver; one spouse may always be the one to deal with your advisor and supply them with information.

TIP

To complete your tax return, give your advisor your savings account statements, and not just a note of the total interest credited in the tax year. If it then transpires that an account which they understood was in the name of one was actually in joint names, they can make the necessary adjustment.

Tax avoidance

Income from jointly-held property for a married couple has to be split on a 50:50 basis. If the source of the funds in the account is other than this, change the basis on which you hold the account, by way of a simple deed.

4.2.5. Pending legislation on income splitting

The Taxman wants to bring in income splitting anti-avoidance provisions to apply whether or not a couple are married. It is not certain that these provisions will become law as currently drafted, but if they do, the business will need to be distributed to the members or shareholders in proportion to effort contributed by each person. For example, a company's share structure may need to be adjusted to achieve this. At least once you are married, gifts of shares between you are made on a no gain, no loss basis, so no CGT tax charge arises.

Tax avoidance

Your respective roles in the family business may change over time. Getting a tax deduction for payments to the person who plays a less active role in the business in the form of salary, benefits, pension contributions or rent, are fine, but dividends or profit shares could be a problem with the Taxman.

4.3. SPOUSE'S SALARY

It's not often that the Taxman offers something for nothing, but there are some free benefits to be had by paying your spouse even a low salary from your business. What are they?

If your business can justify paying only a relatively low salary to your spouse, is it worthwhile doing this, given the extra paperwork and potential hassle from the Taxman? Before giving up on the idea consider the following hidden benefits.

A salary paid above the NI lower earnings limit (LEL) £95 for 2009/10 but below the earnings threshold (ET) (£110 for 2009/10), will not be subject to NI for either the employee or the business.

TIP

There's a bonus in paying a salary pitched between the LEL and the ET. Despite no NI being payable, a full credit for basic state pension will be given as if contributions had been paid.

What about tax? Whether or not tax is payable by your spouse on their salary from your business depends on how much other income they receive. However, paying tax does not detract from the benefit of the free pension credit achieved from paying a salary at the level indicated above.

Example

Mrs X is married to a director of a private company. In 2009/10 she works under a contract of employment for the company - twelve hours per week at £8 per hour - and carries out a variety of functions for the company, ranging from making credit control calls (she can do this from home) to keeping personnel records up-to-date.

Her annual salary is rounded up to £5,000. This is below the ET and so she pays no NI and neither does the business. Also, because she has no other earnings she pays no tax.

The business gets a full deduction for her salary against its profit and Mrs X gets a full year's credit against her NI record that will go towards building up her right to a state pension.

TIP

Even if no NI or tax has been paid, it's vital that your spouse's salary should be put through the payroll system and the end of year certificate of pay and tax deducted (Form P14/P60) produced and submitted to the Taxman. This will ensure that your spouse's NI record is updated with a credit to go towards their pension record.

Trap. If you own two or more businesses, they may be treated as one for NI purposes by the Taxman. Thus, paying your spouse under the NI threshold at, say, £3,000 per annum from two businesses would be treated as a single salary of £6,000, which exceeds the ET and is liable to NI.

Contract of employment

For many reasons it makes good sense to formalise a spouse's employment with your business through an employment contract.

For instance, if your spouse became ill and unable to work, their contract would illustrate continuous employment and so justify a claim for Statutory Sick Pay (SSP) even though, as in the example above, they have paid no NI contributions (see the Download Zone).

Tax avoidance

Paying a salary of just £5,720 (£110 per week for 52 weeks) per annum to your spouse will be free of NI but still earn them a full year's pension credit and qualify them for SSP. Even if your spouse pays no NI or tax, the usual payroll records, P60 etc., must be produced.

Download Zone

For a sample **Spouse's Job Description** setting out their duties, visit **http://books.indicator.co.uk**. You'll find the access code on page 2 of this book.

MPs' expenses

Following requests under the **Freedom of Information Act** (FoIA), it was revealed that several MPs employ family members. And do they stick to the NMW? No. For example, one employed his son (who is a full-time student) on a salary of £950 per month. Others employed their spouses on salaries of between £28,000 and £35,000 p.a., plus pensions and other perks.

TIP

Pay your family member the same as you would a third party (at market rate) for the hours they work. If the Taxman later says this is excessive, remind him how much MPs get away with when paying their families.

4.4. PAYING COMMISSION TO A SPOUSE

What's the problem? You're probably already using the tax-free personal allowance to its full advantage, e.g. as getting the company to pay you and your spouse/partner a tax and NI-free salary of, say, £5,720, either spread over the year or planning a one-off bonus just before the end of the tax year.

The Taxman has long been arguing that "the spouse" should only be paid a derogatory amount for any input into the business, normally this equates to the National Minimum Wage (NMW). Indeed, if you employ any family members then the rate of their remuneration will tend to come under scrutiny during the course of an enquiry into your accounts.

If you employ your spouse or partner, the traditional view is that they should be paid the same amount as you would pay a third party at arm's length; anything higher may be deemed excessive and disallowed for tax as not wholly and exclusively for the purposes of your trade.

Example

A total package of £11,024 works out at just over 37 hours a week at the NMW rate of £5.73 per hour, over 52 weeks. However, your spouse's rate per hour might actually be higher than this. For example, find out the rate per hour an agency would charge to provide cover, e.g. in case of illness, for your spouse's duties for the company. Even after knocking off a percentage from this for the agency's profit margin, you'll end up with a rate higher than the NMW. For example, a rate of £8 an hour would justify a £11,200 package for only 27 hours work a week ((£11,200/£8 per hour = 1,400 hours) /52).

What if your partner actively advertises the business by word of mouth. Are they not then entitled to a commission on every client they introduce to the company? And can that commission not be a percentage of the work done? The answer is "yes" and "yes". As long as the transaction is logged properly, it's difficult for the Taxman to challenge the validity of the payment.

The important point is that whatever you do, document and log everything. Keep a spreadsheet of how the commission calculated has been built up. The Taxman then has to look at your business on the facts unique to it. He cannot rely on his long list of case law to please himself and declare what has been paid to your spouse as being excessive and not related to the trade.

TIP

Calculate commission due to your spouse, for work/clients introduced by them to your business. This will help justify any regular payment they receive from your business. Have different commission rates for different products or services. For example, the referral scheme commission payments offered by one small IT company were 50% of website hosting costs; 15% of Internet marketing services; and 10% of web design and development costs. And no matter how small the project, they'd still make a minimum commission payment of £50.

Download Zone

For a free **Commission for Referrals** document, visit **http://books.indicator.co.uk**. You'll find the access code on page 2 of this book.

4.5. SHARING GAINS

4.5.1. Two annual allowances

Capital Gains Tax (CGT) planning is now a lot less complex since the end of taper relief, which is not available to gains arising after April 5 2008. Every individual has an annual CGT exemption, which in 2009/10 made the first £10,100 of gains free of tax. Gains above the annual exemption are taxed at 18%.

Tax avoidance

Transfers of assets between partners can save CGT when the assets are finally sold.

If one partner has used up the annual exemption and wants to sell more assets, the assets could first be transferred to the other partner so that their annual exemption is used against the gain.

Where assets are held jointly, the gain is split equally and both partners can use their annual exemption.

If one partner has capital losses in 2009/10 or unused losses from earlier years, assets could be transferred to that partner, if the sale of those assets is likely to produce a gain that exceeds the annual exemption.

> **TIP**
>
> Leave as much time as possible between the transfer of the assets and the sale. The Taxman could ignore the effects of the transfer made immediately before a disposal. If documentary proof of ownership of the assets is not available, a deed of gift may be necessary to prove the transfer has taken place.

4.5.2. Tenants-in-common?

Tax avoidance

If you own an asset with your spouse, check whether it's as "joint tenants", meaning you own it equally, or "tenants-in-common" (TIC), which means you can own a defined share, e.g. 20% and 80%. However, the Taxman is allowed to charge tax as if the income is split 50/50 unless he is notified otherwise. Although the TIC arrangement usually applies to property, it can be used for other assets, e.g. shares. A solicitor can alter the terms and proportions of property ownership, whereas you can notify the company registrar direct of any such changes relating to shares.

Trap. The Form 17 procedure can't be used for bank or building society deposits or property being taxed as furnished holiday accommodation.

If you are married or in a civil partnership, you can also give anything you want to your spouse or civil partner and not pay CGT, no matter how valuable it is.

Warning. Bear in mind that if you give something away to your spouse or civil partner, you can't ask for it back. You may save tax but if you split up, you could end up much worse off.

Tax avoidance

Move towards jointly owning assets after you've got married in order to double up on the CGT-free annual allowance when they're sold.

4.5.3. Bed and spousing

Spouses can make unlimited (in size and frequency) no gain/no loss transfers of assets between each other. A recent example of making use of this tax loophole was the banking of indexation relief prior to April 5 2008 by transferring the relevant asset to your spouse.

To bank an existing CGT position you sometimes need to sell your shares before the end of a tax year. But if you still want to hold those shares in the long term, use one of following "bed and breakfast" tricks:

Option 1. Bed and lie-in. After 30 days you buy back the same number of shares. You need to wait for at least 30 days as otherwise your sale and purchase are matched and you can't take advantage of the taper relief. This is a risky strategy as you may have to pay more for the replacement shares if the share price has increased in the 30-day lie-in.

Option 2. Bed and spouse it. Ask your spouse to immediately purchase the same shares, which they can pass to you later in a no-gain, no loss transfer, and pay no tax.

Option 3. Bed and ISA it. Depending on your type of ISA you can ask the fund manager to buy the replacement shares. Or **Bed and SIPP it**. Again, depending on the investment policy of your Self-Invested Pension Plan (SIPP) you can ask the trustees of your SIPP to buy the replacement shares. However, you don't have direct control of the shares with either of these.

Tax avoidance

Where the reduction of tax is the main purpose of undertaking a transaction, the longer the gap between transactions, the more difficult it is for HMRC to associate them.

TIP

Ideally, the gaps between the initial gift and the gift back (and an ultimate disposal) should be as long as possible. Allow, say, three months between transactions, not just the classic 31 days.

TIP

Time the transfer back to match a gift on the occasion of an anniversary, birthday etc. or as part of an estate planning exercise or even in anticipation of a divorce.

TIP

If possible, transfer different assets but to the same value of course.

TIP

There may be a very good reason why the original donor wishes to have the whole of the asset back. However, given that there is a flat-rate of 18% CGT after April 6 2008, consider taking back only one-half of the asset transferred originally. This will enable two (yours and your spouse's) annual exemptions to apply in future on the disposal of the assets.

The new £1 million entrepreneurs' relief and IHT 100% business property relief will need to be considered as the qualifying periods for these may restart each time the assets are gifted. Make sure you raise this question with your tax advisor before embarking on gifting assets to your spouse.

4.6.   ENTREPRENEURS' RELIEF

Both taper relief and indexation allowance were scrapped for all gains made after April 5 2008. This meant small business owners would see a hike in the tax they paid on the sale of their businesses from 10% to 18%. Until…

The new entrepreneurs' relief (ER) can apply when you sell part or all of your business, or shares in your own company after April 5 2008, subject to a gains cap of £1 million. The capital gain will be reduced to 5/9ths of the full gain, making the effective Capital Gains Tax (CGT) rate 10% (5/9 x 18%). So the taper relief position is restored, if all the new relief conditions are met.

Conditions

You must have held the shares or assets for at least a year before the sale, and the business must be trading, so property letting businesses don't qualify. Where you sell a company, you must own at least 5% of the voting ordinary shares, and have either worked in, or been an officer of, the company or an associated company.

Example

You sell the shares in your company for a gain of £450,000. ER reduces the gain to £250,000 (5/9 x £450,000). The tax due is £45,000 (18% x £250,000); an effective rate of 10% on the full gain of £450,000. You can also deduct your annual exemption (£10,100 for 2009/10), and any capital losses from the taxable gain to reduce your tax bill even further.

There is no minimum age limit on ER, so you don't have to "retire" when you sell your business to qualify. But you do need to consider the £1 million cap that can be subject to the relief. This means you can make a number of gains totalling £1 million over several years, and claim ER on them all. Any gains in excess of this will be taxed at the full 18%.

To qualify for ER the shares being sold must be in the owner's personal company. The definition of which is:

- one in which the shareholder owns at least 5% of the ordinary share capital of the company, and as a result can exercise 5% of the voting rights; and

- the owner has been an officer or employee for the twelve months prior to the sale.

If the shareholder hasn't been an employee or officer in the company for the twelve months, they won't qualify for ER, so will attract CGT at 18% not 10%. In our example that's extra tax of £36,000.

Become an officer. Obviously, being a director would qualify as an officer of the company. And just being the company secretary would also help qualify a shareholder for ER. For example, if your spouse also holds shares but doesn't work for the company and isn't already a director, make them company secretary in order for their shareholding to qualify.

Contracts of employment. Make sure you have some form of employment relationship with the company. There is no requirement to be a full-time employee of the company, so part-time jobs or consultancy contracts with the company would suffice. Back this up with contracts of employment and by putting yourself on the payroll.

4.7. ESTATE PLANNING

Couples should have simple wills to avoid problems that can arise on intestacy and to ensure certainty at a time of distress. Any will made prior to marriage will have automatically been revoked on any marriage. Under the intestacy rules a spouse will receive personal chattels, the statutory legacy together with half the residuary estate. The other half would pass to the parents of the deceased.

In the current tax year (2009/10) you have to pay Inheritance Tax (IHT) (or rather the person sorting out your affairs has to pay it out of your estate) if the property and investments etc. that you leave add up to more than £325,000.

This is somewhat of a simplification, because a whole industry has grown up around inventive ways of avoiding IHT. However, you don't need to take out a clever policy; one easy way to beat the Taxman is to get married or enter into a civil partnership.

Your friends and relatives can make IHT-free gifts to either you or your spouse. The limits are £5,000 if the donor is a parent or £2,500 if the donor is a grandparent or great-grandparent. Otherwise, the limit is £1,000.

The marriage invalidates any will in place before the wedding - unless it was evidently written in contemplation of the wedding. So one of the first things you should do on your return from honeymoon is to make a new one. The mess left behind should you die intestate (without a valid will) cannot be over-emphasised, especially if you are the sole director of your company.

The existence of transferable nil-rate bands (the £325,000 threshold for 2009/10) makes IHT planning between married couples easy. A simple will leaving everything to the surviving spouse can now avoid IHT on the first death and maximise the use of both nil-rate bands.

4.8. PENSION CONTRIBUTIONS

Provided their overall package is at a market rate, an employee/director can legitimately have both a salary and a pension contribution paid by their company. As part of the cost of employing staff, pension contributions will be tax deductible for the company.

However, it's worth noting the Taxman's view, which is that the pension contribution is deductible *"in respect of ... an employee who is a close relative ... of the director or if it is comparable with that paid to unconnected employees performing duties of similar value."* So how much pension can your company pay for you to extract profits through this route?

Example

Mr J is a director of a small company, and employs his spouse for general administrative work. A modest salary of £1,200 a year is paid, which is easily commensurate with the duties they carry out. The company also pays an employer contribution into a personal pension scheme for the spouse of £100 per month.

Mr J's pensions advisor is insisting that the company is perfectly entitled to full tax relief on all of the £1,200 annual contributions actually paid and indeed up to the £3,600 annual maximum, irrespective of the salary earned, and is seeking to persuade Mr J's company to increase the pension contributions to the maximum £300 a month (£3,600/12) and obtain maximum CT relief.

The key to this dilemma could rest in the number of years that the spouse has worked for the company without a pension scheme. Because in a similar situation one financial advisor was able to provide figures for a "reasonable" (allowable) level of premiums per annum by taking into account the number of years' service and level of salary paid before the pension scheme commenced. Admittedly this was for an employee pension scheme, however, the same principles apply under the new pensions regime.

> **Tip**
>
> Any amount up to £3,600 a year may be paid as personal pension contributions, but that doesn't mean that the premiums are necessarily tax deductible for the company. Get your advisor to come up with a figure to justify the current pension contribution by taking into account the number of years' service (and salary paid in those years) before this pension arrangement was thought up.

If the annual premium going down this route is not significant, it might be because there hasn't been many years of service pre-pension. So just go with the flow. However, there is something else you could do...

> **Tip**
>
> Link a "one off" pension contribution for the spouse (in our example £3,600 - £1,200 = £2,400) by the company to a year of higher profits and record them as a reward for helping to earn those profits. This should pass the Taxman's "wholly and exclusively" test for tax deductibility. However, don't do this every year.

4.9. PARTNERSHIP LOSSES

A recent announcement by the Taxman of his intention to counter largescale anti-avoidance is actually a reminder of how you could support your spouse in their own business and save yourself tax.

With initial set-up costs etc., many new businesses make a loss in their first year. Let's say your spouse wants to start up a business and you are happy to fund the anticipated losses. In this situation there is a flexible and generous loss relief, which could result in you receiving a substantial tax repayment.

If you set up the new business as a partnership, any loss that the partners make can be offset against their other taxable income, e.g. salary and investment income. Any claim is limited to the capital they've put into the new business. So if your share of the losses is £5,000 and the capital you contributed is £5,000, there is no problem.

As a rule of thumb, as a higher rate taxpayer, your tax repayment would be 40% of the loss figure, e.g. on a £5,000 loss offset against income already taxed at 40%, your tax repayment would be £2,000 (£5,000 x 40%).

Losses in the first four years of trading can be carried back up to three years, earliest year first, against your other income. For example, if the partnership makes a loss in 2009/10 then you could elect to offset this against your income in 2005/6.

TIP

You would only choose to make use of this carry back relief if your top rate of tax was higher three years ago than it is now.

Is it really that simple?

If you're involved in the business for, on average, less than ten hours a week, then you would be considered to be a "non-active" partner meaning the loss relief isn't available.

TIP

Keep detailed records of time spent on partnership affairs. Include meeting and travelling time. Your objective is to get beyond the ten-hour a week benchmark.

TIP

Avoid the ten-hour trap across the whole business by dividing it into two separate manageable functions, for example, manufacture and distribution. You run the one that best fits in with the time you have available or your expertise.

Change 1

The amount of loss relief available to an individual from all partnerships caught by the new provisions will be capped at a maximum £25,000 for any single year.

Change 2

There is also to be a motive test in relation to capital contributions to partnerships. For contributions after March 2 2007 there will be no relief if the main purpose, or one of the main purposes, for contributing the capital to the partnership, is to obtain loss relief.

TIP

If you're not going to put more than £25,000 into a partnership and pass the ten-hour test, you're in the clear.

General

1. Some couples find that one partner pays a higher rate of tax on their income or capital gains while the other does not have enough income to use up their personal allowance and basic rate tax band. The tax avoidance game is therefore to find ways of transferring income and gains between partners in order to take advantage of these otherwise unused allowances and bands.

Sole trader

1. A high income partner with a business could pay their low income partner a salary from that business. A salary of up to £110 per week is both tax and NI-free for 2009/10. However, PAYE records would still need to be kept of this employment.

2. The remuneration must be reasonable in relation to the work done and it must actually be paid to the spouse.

3. As well as salary, a payment could be made as an employer's contribution to a partner's personal pension plan. The partner will not be taxed on this benefit nor will NI be payable on it.

4. Like salary, the pension payments will be deductible from business profits provided the salary and the pension payment combined do not exceed a reasonable rate of remuneration for the work carried out. Excessive pension contributions for a partner or relative may not be deductible on the grounds that they are not wholly and exclusively for the purpose of the trade.

Partnership

1. Profits could be shared by operating the business as a partnership. Both individuals need to be involved in the business, and a written partnership agreement drawn up. Operating as a business partnership will not reduce tax if the business consists of supplying personal services in a form that is caught by the IR35 anti-avoidance legislation.

Limited company

1. If the business is set up as a limited company, and is not a personal service company caught by the IR35 rules, a partner could become a shareholder and receive dividends.

2. An individual who is not liable to higher rate tax has no further tax to pay on dividends.

3. Dividends carry a 10% tax credit that cannot be recovered, so a shareholder needs non-dividend income as well in order to benefit fully from the personal allowance.

Associated companies

1. Companies controlled by individuals who are married are automatically associated for Corporation Tax (CT) purposes, even if there is no commercial link between the businesses. This can lead to increased CT liabilities. However, if one spouse conducts their business through a company and the other is a sole trader they can avoid this potential CT problem.

Splitting investment income

1. Investment income could be transferred by switching the ownership of the asset that produces it. For example, shares could be transferred before a dividend is paid. For this to be effective the asset must be transferred absolutely and unconditionally.

2. In most cases, transferring ownership of assets would generally have its main effect on the income of future years.

3. Transferring assets where the couple is not married or in civil partnership can result in a CGT liability and a potential future Inheritance Tax liability.

4. Transfers of assets between partners who are married or are civil partners are free of CGT and could save on CGT when assets are sold, if one partner has an unused annual exemption or capital losses.

5. Savings could be held in joint names. Normally, each individual is taxable on half the income. This provides scope for transferring income-producing assets without losing complete control.

Sharing gains

1. Transfers of assets between partners can save CGT when the assets are finally sold.

2. If one partner has used up the annual exemption and wants to sell more assets, the assets could first be transferred to the other partner so that their annual exemption of £10,100 is used against the gain.

3. Where assets are held jointly, the gain is split equally and both partners can use their annual exemption.

4. If one partner has capital losses in 2009/10 or unused losses from earlier years, assets could be transferred to that partner, if the sale of those assets is likely to produce a gain that exceeds the annual exemption.

5. Leave as much time as possible between the transfer of the assets and the sale. The Taxman could ignore the effects of the transfer made immediately before a disposal. If documentary proof of ownership of the assets is not available, a deed of gift may be necessary to prove the transfer has taken place.

Entrepreneurs' relief

1. The new entrepreneurs' relief (ER) can apply when you sell part or all of your business, or shares in your own company after April 5 2008, subject to a gains cap of £1 million. The capital gain will be reduced to 5/9ths of the full gain, making the effective CGT rate 10% (5/9 x 18%).

2. Sales of shares are disqualified from ER if the shareholder was not an employee/officer (in the preceding twelve months). So make sure your partner is made a shareholder and employee/officer for that period, e.g. ensure you have a contract.

Estate planning

1. Couples should have simple wills to avoid problems that can arise on intestacy.

2. The existence of transferable nil-rate bands (the £325,000 threshold for 2009/10) makes IHT planning between married couples easy. A simple will leaving everything to the surviving spouse can now avoid IHT on the first death and maximise the use of both nil-rate bands.

Pension contributions

1. Your business can make regular contributions on behalf of your partner as long as it's what other employees might receive or it relates to making up for past years' service. As a one-off it could also pay a performance-related contribution.

Partnership losses

1. With initial set-up costs etc., many new businesses make a loss in their first year. Let's say your partner wants to start up a business and you are happy to fund the anticipated losses. In this situation there is a flexible and generous loss relief, which could result in you receiving a substantial tax repayment.

CHAPTER 5

Property

5.1. INTRODUCTION

The largest capital gain that you are likely to realise is on the disposal of your home. However, you are probably already aware that when you sell your own home, you don't have to pay tax on any gain you make. This exemption from CGT is known as "principal private residence" relief (PPR).

You can still take advantage of this relief to make substantial CGT savings if you don't live in it all the time or even end up owning more than one property. And there are some interesting tax avoidance variations if a buy-to-let property is also involved.

With residential property, tax avoidance starts when you are setting up the deal to buy it. For example, a small difference in the purchase price can make a huge difference to the amount of Stamp Duty Land Tax (SDLT) you pay. How can you legitimately avoid paying SDLT?

During the period you own your home there are concessions to help you with generating some income, say, by taking in a lodger to help with the bills. How can you legitimately avoid paying tax on this income?

If you decide to work from home at some stage in your life, what will the Taxman allow you to claim for against your tax? And is there a problem with maintaining your PPR exemption by using part of your home for a business purpose?

5.2. STAMP DUTY LAND TAX (SDLT)

You have to pay Stamp Duty Land Tax (SDLT) when you purchase a property over a certain price threshold. The rates of SDLT are:

PURCHASE PRICE OF RESIDENTIAL PROPERTY	STAMP DUTY (**)
Up to £175,000(*)	0%
Between £175,001 and £250,000	1%
Between £250,001 and £500,000	3%
Over £500,001	4%

(*) Until December 31 2009. (**) The rate of SDLT remains the same whether you are an individual, partnership, company or trust.

As you can see, a small difference in the purchase price can make a huge difference to the amount of SDLT you pay.

Example

Geoff wants to make an offer on a property of £251,000. If he purchases the property at this price, then the SDLT rate will be 3% and he will therefore pay an additional £7,530. If, however, Paul offers £250,000 for the property, he will only pay SDLT at 1% which would be £2,500. In this case, a purchase price difference of £1,000, gives rise to an additional £5,030 in SDLT.

5.3. FIXTURES AND FITTINGS

Tax avoidance

As you've seen, once the price passes the £250,000 threshold, the amount of SDLT due jumps from 1% to 3%. The seller, on the other hand, doesn't have to pay SDLT, so will want to get as much as possible for their property. The solution would be for you and the seller to come to an agreement whereby the seller prices the property below £250,000 and you pay separately for any fixtures and fittings.

> *Example*
>
> *Peter wishes to purchase a house for £255,000. He offers the vendor £250,000 for the house and £5,000 for carpets, curtains, light fittings, fitted oven, fridge and washing machine. The SDLT he has to pay will be £2,500. If he hadn't paid for the furnishings and fittings separately he would have paid £7,650. He has therefore avoided £5,150 in SDLT. Pricing below £250,000 is, of course, legal, as is negotiating a deal with the seller for furnishings and fittings that takes the actual price paid above £250,000.*

What counts as fixtures and fittings? As a rough guide anything moveable is generally not considered part of the property, and so not subject to SDLT. So if you paid extra for plants in pots, that would be outside SDLT. However, if they were planted in the ground, they would not be moveable and would therefore be considered part of the property. You could also pay separately for carpets, curtains, light fittings, fridges, washing machines, garden furniture and ornaments.

Trap. As a buyer you can face the possibility of an enquiry from the Taxman. This is particularly likely when buying properties at a threshold (known as a "pinch point") where higher rates of tax apply.

> TIP
>
> Make sure you can back up any separate figure you paid for fixtures and fittings. The amount you pay for these should be a reasonable market value. If you've paid well over the odds, then the Taxman will question it.

5.4. RENT-A-ROOM RELIEF

5.4.1. What is tax-free?

If you generate extra income by letting a room in your own home to a lodger, then you can claim a special relief called "rent-a-room" under which you can earn up to £4,250 tax-free. The letting must be for residential purposes and not, for example, used as office accommodation. The lodger will typically have a furnished bedroom and share the use of other rooms, although they could occupy an entire floor of your home.

5.4.2. Gross rent less than £4,250

Tax avoidance

If the total amount you receive in a year from letting part of your house, including charges for meals, cleaning, laundry and goods and services of a similar nature, is less than £4,250, there's no tax to pay. Simply elect for rent-a-room relief to apply by putting an "X" in Box 4 on page UKP1 of the tax return.

TIP

Even if you receive rent-a-room income of less than £4,250 a year (£81 a week), make sure you add up your expenses. If they work out as more than your income, you've made a loss.

Tax avoidance

If you do make a loss on renting out a room, but are renting other property out at a profit, don't apply for the rent-a-room exemption for that particular year of assessment. Instead, include the rental income with your other property income and so offset your loss against those other profits, to pay less tax. If you want to elect not to apply the exemption, don't put an X in Box 4!

Note. A rent-a-room election must be made within twelve months after January 31 following the tax year. For example, for the 2009/10 tax year, an election must be made by January 31 2011, which is also the filing deadline for your tax return.

5.4.3. Gross rent more than £4,250

If your total rent-a-room receipts are more than £4,250, then you will be taxed on your rental income less expenses.

Tax avoidance

However, you can elect to be taxed as if the profit from letting is equal to the difference between total gross rents receivable and £4,250, instead of a deduction for your expenses. If your income is more than £4,250 and your expenses are less than £4,250, then make this election.

Again, it's easy to make the election - don't tick Box 4 on page UKP1 of your tax return. Instead, enter your rental income and the rent-a-room exemption figure £4,250 as your expenses.

Example 1

Jan lets two rooms in her house for £50 a week each (£5,200 a year). She has related expenses of £1,500, so her profit is £3,700. By default Jan will be taxed on her income (£5,200) less expenses (£1,500), £3,700. However, if Jan elects to just be taxed on her rental income over £4,250, then she will only be taxed on £950 (£5,200 - £4,250)

Example 2

Mark lets two rooms in his house for £80 a week each (£8,320 a year). However, he has expenses of £4,800. By default, Mark will be taxed on his income less expenses, i.e. £3,520. If Mark had made an election, he would have been taxed on the higher figure of £4,070 (£8,320 less £4,250.)

5.4.4. Some variations

If you own a property jointly, the £4,250 has to be halved, i.e. £2,125 each. But it's interesting to note that the Taxman hasn't specified what happens if three or more individuals own a house which they all live in. From his guidance, it would seem that each of them has a limit of £2,125.

The rent-a-room relief applies to any proportion of the property that you live in, so renting out more than one room would qualify (as long as each room is furnished). However, the £4,250 tax-free allowance is fixed regardless of the rooms let out. The relief can even extend to the letting of a self-contained flat as long as the division of the property is only temporary.

You must occupy the property as your main home at the same time as the lodger for at least part of the letting period in each tax year. This means that as long as there is some overlap between you living in the property and the lodger being there, you can move out for the rest of the tax year.

You can take advantage of the rent-a-room scheme, regardless of whether you own your own home or rent it. However, if you are renting, you should check whether your lease allows you to take in a lodger.

Download Zone

For a copy of a **Rental Agreement**, visit **http://books.indicator.co.uk**. You'll find the access code on page 2 of this book.

5.5. WORKING FROM HOME

5.5.1. As an employee

If you work at home on a regular basis, what can you claim for? As an employee, you can claim expenses for the costs you incur by working at home. Your employer needs to agree that you will undertake some of your work at home on a regular basis, under a so-called homeworking arrangement (see the Download Zone).

The extra household costs you can claim include the increased energy needed to heat and light the property for longer and the extra water used, if that is metered. However, you can't claim a proportion of your mortgage or Council Tax payments, as these amounts are fixed whether or not you work from home.

When you work at home regularly, but not full-time, your claim for expenses must be made to your employer, not directly to the Taxman. The claim must also be supported by receipts showing the increased energy, water etc. used due to you working at home. These are tedious for you to collect and expensive for your company to process.

Instead of collecting up household bills you can claim a tax-free rate of up to £3 a week from your employer, with no questions asked by the Taxman. No receipts are required from you for expenses being claimed for, and your employer can still pay for things like the cost of business telephone calls, in addition to the weekly rate.

Tax avoidance

If your working at home costs are less than £3 per week, or are too difficult to measure, just ask your employer if they will pay the tax-free rate of £3 per week: £156 per year. However, they can reimburse you for the actual extra energy bills and other costs incurred by working from home if these amount to more than £3 per week.

Download Zone

For a sample **Homeworking Agreement**, visit **http://books.indicator.co.uk**. You'll find the access code on page 2 of this book.

5.5.2. Self-employed

If you run a self-employed business (either part or full-time) from your home, what can you claim for? The Taxman's guidance on the expenses the self-employed can claim whilst working from home, lists particular types of domestic expenditure, which can be apportioned between private and business use. These include mortgage interest, telecommunications cost, insurance and repairs and maintenance. The catch? When a room is not used solely for business purposes, then the proportion of costs that can be claimed is found by dividing time that the room is used for business by the total time period.

Example

An author works for four hours each morning in her living room, which is then also used by the family for four hours in the evening. The room is 10% of the house, so the first step is to take that percentage of the total costs. In apportioning for time, it might optimistically be thought that you compare time spent on business to time spent for other purposes. On this basis the room is used equally for business and leisure, and the costs could be apportioned 50:50. However, the example uses four hours' business in a 24-hour period, so only 4/24 = 1/6 of the costs of the room is claimed.

If it had not been a living room in the example, but instead a study set aside solely for business, then the apportionment would have stopped at the 10% calculation.

(But this would have opened up a Capital Gains Tax bill on the appropriate proportion of the gain on the house when it is sold.)

Tax avoidance

Maximise your use of home deduction that you claim in your self-employed accounts by: **(1)** increasing the range of expenses you currently claim and; **(2)** accurately working out the proportion of these expenses you can claim.

5.5.3. Claiming for your garage

If you have to store, say, product samples for your customers in your own garage, can your business pay for this? Does it make any difference if you are employed or self-employed?

Employed

Any allowance paid by your employer to you for the use of your garage counts as earnings. Therefore, PAYE should be applied to the payment. This will be the case whether or not the garage is attached to your home.

Tax avoidance

Where an employer claims that the payment to an employee is rent chargeable on the employee as property income, then this is tax-deductible for the company and not earnings of the employee. So any payment to you by your employer for use of your garage should be recorded as rent, both in your company's books as an expense and on your own tax return as income. However, on your return you now get to claim for any additional costs of meeting your company's requirements for the safe-keeping etc. of that stock whilst in your garage.

> **TIP**
>
> Back up the rental claim with a formal licence agreement between you and your employer setting out the terms and conditions of this rental agreement. Include the additional measures your company expects you to take over preserving the condition of the stock (use the list given for the self-employed as a guide to what you could include).

Download Zone

For a sample **Licence Agreement**, visit **http://books.indicator.co.uk**. You'll find the access code on page 2 of this book.

Self-employed

Let's say you have to store product samples for your customers (you act as a self-employed sales rep for a number of clients) and use your own garage for this storage. You'd have to rent somewhere else for this purpose if you didn't use your own garage. Is it possible to claim some storage costs in addition to the costs claimed for using your home as an office?

You should easily be able to come up with the additional costs incurred wholly and exclusively by using your garage for storage. Here are eight to get you started: **(1)** some products must not be exposed to high or low temperatures, so a proportion of household electricity costs to cover use of a heater in winter or a fan in summer should be claimed; **(2)** any storage boxes/cages; **(3)** additional insurance premiums; **(4)** security measures - from a more secure door, through to sensor activated lights to an alarm system; **(5)** additional lighting; **(6)** weather proofing; **(7)** smoke alarm, fire extinguisher, sand bucket (particularly for chemical spills) etc. and; **(8)** the cost of a trolley to move products to and from the car/van - health and safety must be observed at all times.

Tax avoidance

As self-employed, if you already claim "use of home as office", include the garage as an additional room for apportioning costs between business and non-business. Also, claim for costs directly related to providing that storage.

5.6. PRINCIPAL PRIVATE RESIDENCE (PPR) RELIEF

5.6.1. Tax avoidance

You can avoid CGT on a property if it has, at some time, been classed as your only or main residence. If the property was your only or main home throughout your period of ownership, then you can automatically claim full PPR relief and so you have no CGT liability. This is regardless of the capital gain you make on the property.

In fact, the property doesn't have to be your main home for the entire period of ownership in order to avoid significant amounts of CGT. Yes, certain periods of absence don't count but any period of occupancy does. The amount of relief you can claim is calculated by dividing the total time, e.g. in months, that it was your PPR by the total length of time, again, say, in months, that you owned the property.

Three-year bonus

Three years of absence, for any reason whatsoever, are ignored. This can be a single period of three years or shorter periods as long as they don't add up to more than three years in total.

Example 1

William moves in with his partner and lets his own property to pay the mortgage etc. on it. He's also waiting for the market to pick up before selling it. If he sells the property within three years of it ceasing to be his main residence, he can have that period of absence ignored for CGT purposes and so not pay any CGT on the sale.

Example 2

Wayne buys a home in May 1994 for £70,000. He lives there until July 1996 before moving to a bigger home nearby. Wayne eventually sells his original house in June 2004 for £150,000.

The house was Wayne's main residence for 26 months and he owned the property for a total of 121 months. Therefore, the house is treated as being Wayne's PPR for 62 months (the 26 months he actually lived there plus the last 36 months) and the actual relief claimed is 62/121ths.

What is left is his taxable gain (before any annual CGT exemption is deducted is £39,008 (59/121ths of £80,000)).

Warning. Relief is denied if your acquisition was made wholly or partly with a view to realising a gain. While on a strict interpretation of the law this could be held to apply to nearly all property, the Taxman normally only attacks those who buy and sell in quick succession.

5.6.2. Evidence of residence

The Taxman hasn't issued any specific guidance on this, but obviously, the longer you live in the property the better chance you have of claiming PPR relief. However, the Taxman is more interested in whether the property really was your home and whether you did live there rather than a length of time; quality of occupation he calls it. So the more evidence you have that it was your main residence, the more likely you are to convince him.

TIP

To back up your claim for main residence (should the Taxman query it) then:

- change your address with your local tax office. So, even his records show that the relevant property was your main residence!

- put utility bills in your own name at the property address. Typical bills include gas, electricity, water, Council Tax and TV licence

- register on the voters roll at the property

- change your address with your bank, so that all statements are delivered to that property address

- hire a removal van to move enough furniture from one house to the house you want to be your main residence. Keep receipts for any new furniture delivered to the property

- don't advertise the property for sale or rent until after the period of residence

- have building work at your main home so you have to move out. Therefore, you can prove that you must be residing at the "investment" property.

5.7. SWITCHING YOUR PPR

5.7.1. Making an election

An unmarried individual or a married couple can only have one main residence for PPR relief at any one time. So if you end up owning more than one property at the same time, you will pay CGT on at least one of them when you sell.

However, if you've got more than one home, it is possible to nominate which one you would like to be treated as your PPR. By doing this, it's possible to minimise the tax charge on both properties by switching PPR between them.

The election must be made in writing to the Taxman and sent to your tax office. In the case of a couple, both partners must sign the election for it to be effective.

5.7.2. Timing

From the date of purchasing or acquiring the other property, you have two years to tell the Taxman which one is your PPR.

Tax avoidance

You can extend the two-year time limit by renting a flat for a few months as a third residence. Then you can elect one of the three properties within two years of starting to rent the flat.

5.7.3. Changing the election

Once you've nominated a PPR, you can change it by making a similar election in writing to the Taxman. The new election can be backdated by up to two years.

Tax avoidance

When making a PPR election, choose the property that is most likely to make a bigger capital gain or be sold first. If you do end up selling the other one first, then you simply change the election before selling it.

Download Zone

For a sample **Nominating a Residence Election**, visit **http://books.indicator.co.uk**. You'll find the access code on page 2 of this book.

5.8. PRIVATE LETTING RELIEF

If you let your main residence or part of it as residential not commercial accommodation, then you can claim private letting relief. It makes no difference whether you let the property out before or after it became your main residence.

The amount of private letting relief you can claim is the lower of:

- the amount of PPR relief

- £40,000

- the gain before letting relief is set off (i.e. this relief can't create a capital loss).

> *Example*
>
> *Nick bought a house in August 2002 for £100,000 and lived in it as his main residence for one year. He then moved out and let the property for five years before selling it in August 2009 for £240,000. Nick can claim PPR for 48 months (the twelve months he lived there plus the last thirty six months) of the 72 months he owned the property. Therefore £46,667 of the gain is potentially taxable. However, Nick can claim maximum letting relief of £40,000 (the PPR is £100,000) reducing his gain to just £6,667, he can offset the annual exemption of £10,100 for the 2009/10 tax year, so he ends up with no tax to pay.*

By living in the property for one year after he first acquired it, Nick has made a tax-free gain of £140,000 (£240,000 - £100,00), a tax saving of £25,200 (CGT at 18% of £140,000).

Tax avoidance

If you put the property into joint names, the husband and wife or registered civil partners can each claim private letting relief. That's a potential £80,000 worth of gain that you can avoid CGT on.

5.9. SOME VARIATIONS

5.9.1. Scenario one

Trap. If you invest in a buy-to-let property, let and sell it, it will never have been your main residence. If the property has never been your home, then you miss out on claiming both PPR and private letting relief on any capital gain you make.

TIP

Instead of investing in a buy-to-let property, let out the house that has been your main residence and move into a new property.

Tax avoidance

As the let property was once your main residence, the last three years of ownership are exempt from CGT. So, if you sell the property within three years then you automatically have no tax to pay. If the property is sold after more than three years, then private letting relief can reduce (or even eradicate) the capital gain.

5.9.2. Scenario two

Trap. You already own an investment property that you have let out for a number years. You never lived in the property so you will be unable to claim both PPR and private letting relief. Therefore you are facing a hefty CGT bill when you sell the property.

TIP

Make sure you live in the previously let property before you sell.

Tax avoidance

By making the property your main residence for only a short time, not only can you claim PPR, but you can claim private letting relief too.

5.10. GARDENS AND GROUNDS

Is the garden to your house also covered by the PPR exemption? It depends, is the answer. If you sell land that is part of your main residence, e.g. part of the garden or grounds, the Taxman might take a cut of the proceeds by way of CGT. In this case size is everything.

5.10.1. Half a hectare

If the total area of the garden is less than half a hectare (just over an acre), then the Taxman will readily accept the land as being part of your main residence. Therefore, you will be able to claim full PPR and any gain will be exempt from CGT.

Tax avoidance

If the property was your home and has subsequently been let as a private residential accommodation, then you can still claim partial PPR and private letting relief where the garden is less than half a hectare.

5.10.2. More than half a hectare

If you've got more than half a hectare of grounds, you should argue an increase in area that's classed as garden so that a larger area can be argued as CGT-exempt. A number of taxpayers have tried to extend the limit to reflect the size and character of their homes. The argument being that a larger area is required for the reasonable enjoyment of a larger house. Some have been successful, some not. If you manage to increase an exempt area, you also reduce the taxable area. If you think a bigger area is appropriate, then try to negotiate this with the Taxman.

Trap. If you sell your main residence before you sell the land, then you are unable to claim PPR on the sale of the land.

Tax avoidance

So you don't lose your PPR exemption sell the land before you sell the house and remaining garden. And don't fence off the development plot until it is sold.

5.11. MAKING USE OF YOUR CHILDREN

Every individual can have a main residence and this includes your children. And if they have a main residence, they will be entitled to claim PPR when they sell the property.

If you have children going away to college or university, then you may want to buy them a house nearby as both an investment for their future and somewhere semi-decent for them to live. If you decide to do this, make sure it is structured correctly to make maximum use of various reliefs.

The property should be purchased in your child's name. There shouldn't be any problem getting finance for this as long as you are prepared to put down the deposit to act as guarantor on the mortgage.

As long as it's your child's only property, it will be regarded as their main residence and PPR will be available on the sale of it.

Tax avoidance

As long as you give the mortgage deposit to your child with no strings attached and they are not contractually obligated to give you a share of the proceeds, then there is no reason why they can't make a generous cash gift to you once they have sold the property.

5.12. JOINT OWNERSHIP

In England and Wales a couple can own property either as "joint tenants" when they both own an equal interest in the whole property, or as "tenants-in-common" where each own separate and identifiable shares. Which of these will save you the most tax?

5.12.1. Shared ownership

You'll probably buy your first investment property in your sole name. However, buying property jointly can have significant tax savings. This can be owning a property jointly, with your spouse or with someone else. If you decide to own a house jointly with someone else (whether it's your spouse, partner, relative or friend), you can own it in one of two ways - as joint tenants or tenants-in-common.

If you decide to transfer a property to your spouse (or anyone else for that matter), then you will need to let your solicitor know what type of joint ownership you want. The legal terms used to describe different types of ownership make reference to "tenants". This makes it seem as though it's about rented property. That is not the case - it's just legal jargon!

Joint tenants

Here, the joint owners do not have particular shares in the property; they own the whole thing together. When one owner dies, the property automatically becomes the possession of the other owner(s), because no joint owner has a defined share, their interest in the property does not become part of their estate when they die, but simply disappears. This means that a will made by the first tenant to die, which leaves the property to someone else, would be ineffective.

A husband and wife are normally treated as owning joint property as joint tenants so they have equal rights over the property and when one dies, the other automatically owns it.

If you own a property as joint tenants, then your capital gains will be divided equally between you. As would any rental profits if you were to rent the property out.

Tenants-in-common

Each owner has a defined share of the property. They can decide between themselves what proportion of the property belongs to each owner. When the property is sold, each owner is entitled to his or her percentage share. If one of the owners dies, their share is added to their estate and does not automatically pass to the other tenants-in-common.

Note. If you don't specify that you want a different proportion, then the law assumes that the shares are equal, i.e. if there are two owners, this will automatically be half each, if three owners, a third each and so on.

It's only if you and your spouse own a property in unequal shares as tenants-in-common, that you can elect to have your rental profits split in the proportion of your ownership. Any capital gain will automatically be divided between you according to your proportion of ownership.

Which method should you use?

Joint tenants is most suitable for you and your spouse where the combined value of your properties is likely to be under two times the Inheritance Tax (IHT) threshold, i.e. under £650,000 for 2009/10. If you have a main residence and separate buy-to-let investment properties, this may not be the case.

Tenants-in-common is a more suitable form of ownership when:

- you are not married to other owners, e.g. family, friends, business associates, unmarried partners; or

- the combined value of you and your spouse's property is over twice the IHT threshold, i.e. over £650,000 for 2009/10; or

- you need to have unequal shares in a property, for example to save on income tax on rents.

Note. You may be able to change from joint tenants-in-common at a later date, but you will not be able to change back from tenants-in-common to joint tenants.

5.12.2. Making changes

If you currently own the property as joint tenants, then it is relatively simple to change to tenants-in-common. However, we would recommend that you seek advice from a solicitor before doing this.

Consider the consequences of severing a joint tenancy carefully. If you are actually living in the property and choose to sever the tenancy, the death of your partner could mean you are prematurely forced to sell your house. You will not automatically receive your partner's share in the property should he or she die, as would have been the case had the joint tenancy been preserved.

This can, of course, be overcome by making sure that your partner's share in the property is left to you in their will, but you may not want to do this for IHT reasons. In the past few years it has been a popular way to ensure that the nil-rate band of the first spouse to die is utilised as they passed their shares to, say, their children. However, since the changes to the IHT rules for spouses, it may no longer be advisable to do so. Always seek professional advice before doing this.

KEY POINTS

Stamp Duty Land Tax (SDLT)

1. Once the price of a property passes an SDLT threshold, the amount you pay as a buyer increases. The solution would be for you and the seller to come to an agreement whereby the seller prices the property below the threshold and you pay separately for any fixtures and fittings.

2. Make sure you can back up any separate figure you paid for fixtures and fittings. The amount you pay for these should be a reasonable market value. If you've paid well over the odds, then the Taxman will question it.

Rent-a-room relief

1. If you rent out a room in your own home to a lodger, then you can claim a special tax relief which allows you to earn up to £4,250 tax-free.

2. If your income is more than £4,250 but your expenses are less than £4,250, elect to be taxed on the difference between total gross rents receivable and £4,250, instead of a deduction for your expenses.

3. You must occupy the property as your main home at the same time as the lodger for at least part of the letting period in each tax year. This means that as long as there is some overlap between you living in the property and the lodger being there, you can move out for the rest of the tax year.

Working from home

1. As an employee if your working at home costs are less than £3 per week, or are too difficult to measure, just ask your employer if they will pay the tax-free rate of £3 per week: £156 per year. However, they can reimburse you for the actual extra energy bills and other costs incurred by working from home if these amount to more than £3 per week.

2. If self-employed and working from home, maximise your use of home deduction that you claim in your self-employed accounts by increasing the range of expenses you currently claim.

3. As self-employed, if you already claim "use of home as office", include the garage as an additional room for apportioning costs between business and non-business. Also, claim for costs directly related to providing that storage.

4. Any allowance paid by your employer to you for the use of your garage counts as earnings. Therefore PAYE should be applied to the payment.

Principal private residence relief (PPR)

1. You can avoid Capital Gains Tax (CGT) on a property if it has at some time been classed as your only or main residence. If the property was your only or main home throughout your period of ownership, then you can automatically claim full PPR relief and so you have no CGT liability.

2. Married couples can only have one residence between them.

3. The property doesn't have to be your main home for the entire period of ownership in order to avoid CGT.

4. Make sure the facts about your occupancy of a property fit the description of it as your main residence.

5. Each time you acquire another residence (without having sold the old one) inform the Taxman which one you want to be treated as your main one.

6. Choose the property that is most likely to make a bigger capital gain or be sold first as your main residence. If you do end up selling the other one first, then you simply change the election back before selling it.

7. Care should be taken if the property is bought with a view to resale as the PPR exemption may be jeopardised.

Private letting relief

1. If you let your main residence or part of it as residential not commercial accommodation, then you can claim up to £40,000 private letting relief.

2. If you put the property into joint names, the husband and wife or registered civil partners can each claim private letting relief. That's a potential £80,000 worth of gain that you can avoid CGT on.

Gardens and grounds

1. If the total area of the garden is less than half a hectare (just over an acre), then the Taxman will readily accept the land as being part of your main residence. Therefore, you will be able to claim full PPR relief as any gain will be exempt from IHT.

2. If the property was your home and has subsequently been let as private residential accommodation, then you can still claim partial PPR relief and private letting relief where the garden is less than half a hectare.

3. If you sell your main residence and remaining garden/grounds before you sell the plot of land, then you won't be able to claim PPR relief on the later sale. So sell the house first.

Making use of your children

1. Every individual can have a main residence and this includes your children. And if they have a main residence, they will be entitled to claim PPR relief when they sell the property.

2. The property should be purchased in your child's name with you acting as the guarantor on the mortgage. As long as you give the mortgage deposit to your child with no strings attached and they are not contractually obligated to give you a share of the proceeds, then there is no reason why they can't make a generous cash gift to you once they have sold the property, tax-free.

Joint ownership variations

1. In England and Wales a couple can own property either as "joint tenants" when they both own an equal interest in the whole property, or as "tenants-in-common" where each own separate and identifiable shares.

2. Joint tenants is most suitable for you and your spouse where the combined value of your properties is likely to be under two times the Inheritance Tax (IHT) threshold.

3. Tenants-in-common is a more suitable form of ownership when you are not married to other owners.

CHAPTER 6

Relationship breakdown

6.1. INTRODUCTION

Couples can build up substantial value in assets together, ranging from bank accounts to houses. When these are divided at the end of a relationship there could be tax consequences. During a break up the last thing on your mind is likely to be the Capital Gains Tax (CGT) implications of your actions. What are the traps concerning the joint assets, e.g. the matrimonial home, and how can they be avoided?

Having decided to go your separate ways, one of the last financial aspects to be sorted out could be ownership of shares in the family company. However, if you leave this to the last minute there could be CGT to pay.

One tax question you both may not have thought of is who will get custody of the tax records?

6.2. MATRIMONIAL HOME

With the potential redistribution of jointly held assets, a tax burden can often be added at an already difficult time. However, putting in the right claims to the Taxman can get round this problem.

6.2.1. Principal private residence (PPR)

The concept of PPR is one of these tax saving claims. In a nutshell, the home you live in is free from Capital Gains Tax (CGT) on disposal, and with divorce this is still the case. So if the home has to be sold as part of a settlement, or one party's share has to be transferred to the other, the disposal is free from CGT providing the transfer is done at the right time.

Second, or further properties, can make the situation more complicated. If the relevant tax elections have not been made, then a settlement could see properties transferred that do not have PPR status and which therefore could attract significant gains.

Tax avoidance

Transfers of assets between husband and wife or vice versa are exempt from CGT. This could be crucial if a settlement is reached without a formal divorce taking place. However, the exempt status is available only to married couples who live together. The status is lost at the end of the tax year in which a couple formally separate, so they have to make the most of this whilst they still live together, making interim settlements of assets between them.

6.2.2. Using the second home

If you can't stand to live together under the same roof, it would be a good idea for one of you to establish some deemed occupation in an otherwise non-PPR property, e.g. your holiday home. This means that gains are time apportioned between their taxable and non-taxable elements.

However, to be eligible for this status it is necessary for the property to have been occupied as the PPR at some time, even if that period is as short as, say, one month. **(Note.** The last 36 months are tax-free if the property has been a PPR at any time.**)**

Tax avoidance

One of the parties should go and live in the property they expect to transfer or sell, not the one they expect to keep. For example, they should go and live in the jointly owned buy-to-let/holiday home and if necessary pay market rent to the other spouse on the half they do not own. This will allow half to escape CGT for the last 36 months of ownership.

Tip

Make sure you tell the authorities of your change of address, so that they have it on record should the Taxman query it.

Tip

PPR election is by letter to the Taxman, not through your respective tax returns. This has the advantage of making the system simpler and easier to administer, but puts the onus on you to make the claim (within two years). The Taxman won't phone you up to check that you've claimed enough CGT relief!

6.3. INVESTMENTS

Couples hopefully build up substantial value in assets together ranging from bank accounts to houses. When these are divided at the end of a relationship there could be tax consequences.

Example

Some years before their marriage ended, Mr A bought a commercial property that he let. As part of usual tax planning wisdom he transferred a half share of the property to his wife who, having no other income, could receive her share of the rent at lower rates of tax.

They separated in August 2005, at which time the property value was nearly £200,000 more than the original cost. As part of the divorce settlement Mr A transferred his share of the property to Mrs A. They agreed to this arrangement in May 2006.

The Taxman demanded nearly £30,000 Capital Gains Tax (CGT) saying that he deemed Mr A had sold his share of the property to Mrs A at market value which resulted in a large capital gain even though he had not received a penny.

Even though a couple may be separated, they are considered to be "connected persons" by the Taxman until they are divorced, i.e. the decree absolute is issued. Special tax anti-avoidance rules apply to connected persons so that, whether any money changes hands or not, any transfer of assets between them is treated as if it were a sale at full market value.

Tax avoidance

If you and your spouse intend to separate, don't do it close to the end of the tax year, e.g. if you separate on March 31, any transfer of assets between you after April 5 but before you are divorced will be deemed to be a sale at market value.

TIP

If time is short but you know some of the assets you intend to transfer between you, agree this in a contract by the April 5 following your separation, as for CGT purposes the contract date is the date of transfer. Transfer or agree a contract to transfer the assets between you by April 5 following your separation.

6.4.   SHARES IN THE FAMILY COMPANY

6.4.1.   The problem

Having decided to go your separate ways, one of the financial aspects yet to be sorted out is the family company. If you leave this to the last minute, there could be Capital Gains Tax to pay. So what should you do?

Suppose you run the business, but for historical reasons your spouse owns a substantial block of shares in the company. After the divorce, you would like a clean break and not to have your spouse owning any part of the company.

You could leave the share ownership/valuation issue to be resolved as part of the overall divorce settlement. This is likely to take some time (could be years) but if you wait that long, you could end up with a potential CGT liability.

Example

It's now a couple of years down the line, you are not living together any more and the divorce agreement is about to be finalised. If your spouse now transfers their shares to you as part of the "financial settlement", the Taxman will say that they have disposed of their shares and realised a profit for CGT purposes based on the "current market value" of the shares.

Suppose your spouse's shares are now worth £100,000 - even if valued just using the net assets of the company rather than future profits. They originally cost only £1 each when you set up the company, so the Taxman will expect her to pay CGT on this substantial gain at her highest rate of tax - likely to be 40%. So your spouse is left with an immediate tax bill and so would seek a further settlement to recompense them.

6.4.2. No gain/no loss transfers

Transfers between husband and wives are, for CGT purposes, treated as having been made on a "no gain, no loss" basis, i.e. no tax to pay. But you have to be "living together" to get this. In our example, because the settlement has taken so long you are no longer living together and so can't take advantage of the concession. But there is another way to go about this.

The transfer between husband and wife rule applies to transfers made in a tax year during any part of which a husband and wife are living together.

TIP

Get your spouse to transfer their shares in the company to you before the end of the tax year (April 5) in which you are still living together. This way it will be treated as a no gain, no loss transfer. The date on the share transfer form will be evidence of when this actually happened. You might feel it's unrealistic to be able to agree anything with your spouse at this stage, but common ground may well be the way to beat the Taxman.

TIP

Don't let sorting out the other financial aspects of the divorce delay this transfer of shares. Agree between you that their "value" will be taken into account in the final settlement. This should be done in the form of a legal document drawn up by your solicitors.

Tax avoidance

Keep the Taxman out of the divorce by making transfers of assets whilst you are still regarded as living together - it can be hard enough to split everything two ways, let alone three! Don't wait until the final settlement otherwise you could end up with a CGT bill to settle.

6.4.3. Holdover relief

With a divorce it may well be that nothing is done about the shares in the family company until a final settlement is reached, which is likely to take some time. At that point one of the spouses may transfer their shares to the other as part of the financial agreement between them. One may dispose of their shares to the other and make a profit. The Taxman will expect CGT to be paid on that profit.

CGT holdover relief exists for business assets (such as the shares) so that the tax liability is effectively deferred until the receiving spouse comes to sell the asset.

However, the argument that the Taxman might use runs like this. Holdover relief only applies to gifts or to disposals at undervalue. However, if one spouse passes their shares to the other as part of the divorce settlement, it will be anything but a gift. There will have been some hard negotiating elsewhere in the financial arrangements. In short, the transfer is not a gift, but is made for full consideration!

Solution 1

Transfers between a husband and wife living together are, for CGT purposes, made on a no-gain, no-loss basis. In other words, tax-free. In practice of course, the spouses may no longer be living together. However, this rule applies to transfers made in the tax year during any part of which a husband and wife are living together.

If one of the spouses transfers their shares before the end of the tax year (April 5) there would be no prospect of the Taxman taking CGT on the gain (less taper relief). No doubt the spouses would agree that this is a premature transfer - i.e. before all other aspects had been sorted out, it would need to be taken into account in the final reckoning.

Solution 2

Holdover relief where shares are transferred under a court order. The Taxman now accepts that where assets are transferred between divorcing parties under a court order, it doesn't count as consideration for anything.

> TIP
>
> Use solution 1 wherever possible. However, if the couple run out of time and miss the April 5 deadline for the tax-free transfer, then…

As a second choice use solution 2. Ensure that the transfer of shares is made under a court order (or have it formally ratified by the court) and jointly elect for holdover relief. In this way the Taxman is kept out of the equation.

Tax avoidance

Ensure that the transfer of shares is made under a court order and jointly elect for holdover relief. In this way the Taxman can now be kept out of the divorce equation on a transfer of shares in the family company.

6.5.　TAX RECORDS

Make sure you keep copies of all your tax records. This includes a copy of all agreements and court orders related to the divorce. Can you imagine asking a disgruntled ex-spouse for a copy of your tax records when you are facing an enquiry?

TIP

In practice, the Taxman can only easily enquire into your return within two years of the date the return in question was filed. However, if you have property or don't file a return, keep your records for no less than seven years.

Property records

If you hold property for an extended period of time, you absolutely must keep records relating to it for longer than the enquiry window into a return. (This is particularly true if you own buy-to-let.) If you purchased a property for £100,000 and make an additional £20,000 of capital improvements over the years, you must keep records for the day when you sell the property. You need to retain proof of the total amount you have spent on the property including the cost of later improvements so you can show these figures to the Taxman if he ever asks.

TIP

Keep all your property records for a period of no less than seven years after the tax year in which the property is sold.

6.6.　MAINTENANCE PAYMENTS

Since April 6 2000, no tax relief has been available for pre- or post-1998 maintenance payments or recipients of maintenance payments. It's no longer attractive from a tax viewpoint to arrange for maintenance payments to be paid to a child of the marriage (although a parent may wish to make maintenance payments to the child for other reasons).

As there will be no tax advantage in providing school fees by way of court order, the parent may prefer to receive invoices from and make payments to the school direct.

Where one of the parties was over 65 on April 5 2000, the payer can continue to obtain relief at 10% up to a maximum payment of £2,280.

6.7. PENSIONS

The **Pensions Act 1995** requires courts to take account of the value of private pension benefits in all divorce cases coming before them after July 1 1996. The key aspects of the **Welfare Reform and Pensions Act 1999** include:

1. The option of pension sharing on divorce or nullity of marriage.

2. The financial settlement on divorce will allow pension rights to be transferred in whole or in part between spouses.

3. Retaining the offset of pension rights against other assets.

4. Continuing with earmarking and attachment arrangements if preferred.

5. Applying only to divorce or nullity proceedings commenced after the legislation was brought into force on December 1 2000.

Offsetting

This is a clean break option which provides the ex-spouse with cash compensation for a lost pension entitlement.

Earmarking

This means waiting for a share of the ex-spouse's pension on retirement. However, if the spouse dies before retiring, there may be no pension to pay over.

Sharing

This is the most radical option as it allows the ex-spouse to take a share of the pension pot and either set up a personal pension plan, or use the funds to become a shadow member of the spouse's pension fund. The spouse who gives up a proportion of the pension fund, post April 2006 will now be able to make good lost pension contributions. However, the pension credit will count towards the recipient's standard personal allowance. The divorcing couple will also face charges estimated to be up to £1,200 to carve up the pension scheme.

The government envisages that most pensions will be split equally, but the court will decide, taking into consideration other assets. Once the division has been decided, the scheme must implement the carve-up within four months. The basic state pension is not affected by these rules.

The level of the ex-spouse's state pension will depend upon their own contribution record and part of their former spouse's record. The ex-spouse can use the contributions of their former spouse for all the tax years falling within the marriage, or the period beginning with the start of their working life, and ending with the divorce, whichever is more favourable. Make enquiries of the DSS as to the ex's prospective pension, and consideration should be given to its possible increase by paying class 3 voluntary contributions.

KEY POINTS

1. Where possible, any rearrangement of assets should take place within the tax year of separation.

2. If a charge to CGT is likely to arise as a result of complying with the terms of the financial settlement and the decree absolute is due early in a tax year, tax can be saved if you both agree that part of the transfer is made by agreement before the end of the previous tax year, thereby using two years' exemptions available to the transferor.

3. There is no limit to the IHT exemption applying to transfers between UK domiciled spouses but it is lost when the decree becomes absolute. A transfer by agreement prior to the decree absolute should be considered. Failing this, you can rely on a provision which allows transfers for the maintenance of an ex-spouse to be exempt.

4. This is also the opportunity for each of your wills to be rewritten to take advantage of the latest in tax saving thinking.

5. Before you officially move out of the matrimonial home, transfer assets between you ahead of a final agreement in order to save on CGT. And consider moving out to your holiday home when you do go.

CHAPTER 7

Maximising income

7.1. INTRODUCTION

Recommencement of a spouse's career, and/or higher earnings of the other spouse possibly present an opportunity to save and invest surplus income. Obviously, a balance will need to be achieved to provide liquidity in the event of children's unexpected costs. If you have decided to invest in property, how can you avoid tax on your letting income.

You'll need to generate as much income as possible as this stage will probably involve a period of continuing maintenance for children, particularly if they go on to further education. Is there any way the tax rules could help you with the cost of this?

If you have surplus income, there are some tax advantages to making gifts.

7.2. RENTAL INCOME

If you invest in property, you have to pay income tax on any rental profit (income less expenses) you make during the tax year. The amount you pay depends on your total income from all sources for the year. As with any other business, you are able to offset property-related expenditure against the gross rents you receive. Therefore, to reduce your rental profit and, consequently, the amount of tax you pay, you need to claim as many expenses as possible.

7.2.1. Interest charges

Buying a property to rent usually involves some level of borrowing. You can offset the interest paid on these loans against your rental income. The general rule is that you can claim interest on any loans that are incurred for the purposes of the property investment. Whether the loan interest is an allowable deduction doesn't depend on which property the loan is secured on, but rather what the funds are used for.

Tax avoidance

As you can't get relief on a loan to buy your own property, aim to borrow as much as possible (with interest-only loans) against your investment properties and use the rental profits to pay off the mortgage on your own property. That way you will get tax relief on all your borrowings.

7.2.2. Structural repairs and maintenance costs

The Taxman's general rule is that you can claim any expenses that "prevent the property from deteriorating". This means that you can't offset the costs of any improvements you make to the property against your rental income. The distinction between repairs and improvements is a grey area.

Note. Any improvement costs that you can't offset against your rental income can be offset against your capital gain when you sell the property.

Tax avoidance

Instead of spending a huge amount on a property all at once, you undertake a rolling programme of improvement. This is more likely to be allowed as a repair and therefore "revenue expenditure".

TIP

Claim the following "structural" costs against your rental income:

- exterior and interior painting
- damp and rot treatment
- replacing roof tiles/slates and guttering
- re-pointing
- mending broken windows
- stone cleaning.

TIP

When you are having structural work done to a property, ask the builder for a fully itemised invoice so that you can easily identify the allowable repair costs.

Tax avoidance

Replace old material with the "modern equivalent" to get a deduction from your rental income. For example, double glazing is the modern equivalent of single glazing, and replacing wooden beams with steel girders or lead pipes with copper or plastic would be an allowable deduction.

7.2.3. Renewing fixtures and fittings

Fixtures and fittings are items that are attached to the property and generally cannot be removed without causing damage to it. They would include: radiators, light fittings, kitchen units, baths, wash basins and toilets. What if you wanted to, say, put in a new kitchen or bathroom in a property that you've already let out?

Tax avoidance

Keep to replacing "like-for-like" to get a tax deduction against your rental income and avoid the cost being classed as capital to be added to the cost of the property. For example, if you spend £4,000 replacing a worn out bathroom suite (bath, washbasin and toilet) on a "like-for-like" basis, you can claim the whole lot against your rental income.

TIP

When you are having refurbishment work done, ask for a fully itemised invoice so you can easily prove the like-for-like replacements.

7.2.4. Renewing furniture and furnishings

Unfortunately, you cannot claim the initial cost of furnishing a property against your rental income. Furniture and furnishings are effectively moveable items and include: beds, sofas, table and chairs, curtains and carpets and white goods such as a washing machine or freezer.

Tax avoidance

There are two ways you can claim for the cost of renewing these items. You can either claim the actual cost of buying replacement furniture or you can claim a "wear and tear allowance". You cannot claim both. The wear and tear allowance (10% of rents less water rates and Council tax paid by you) is very generous and will, therefore, usually work out to be more beneficial than claiming the actual cost of replacement furniture. Also, you can start claiming the allowance as soon as you have rental income rather than wait until you replace furniture at some point in the future.

TIP

Make sure you rent the property with just enough furniture to qualify as fully furnished so that you can claim the wear and tear allowance. The cost of second hand furniture is very low compared to the tax savings you could make.

Tax avoidance

The wear and tear allowance only applies to furnishings, so claim for the cost of repairs to fixtures and fittings as well.

7.2.5. Capital allowances

As a landlord, you may have had to purchase equipment and machinery wholly and exclusively for managing your properties. These items are likely to last more than one year.

Tax avoidance

Use the annual investment allowance for your property letting business to claim 100% of the cost (up to £50,000) of equipment and machinery used wholly and exclusively for managing your properties, against your rental income. Claim for office equipment, such as a computer, which you use to keep your rental records, as well as machinery for maintenance of the property, such as a carpet cleaner or a drill.

7.2.6. Travelling costs

You might have to travel to your investment property to carry out maintenance and repairs and viewings with prospective tenants. What costs can you claim?

Tax avoidance

If you are travelling by car, claim a tax-free mileage allowance of 40p per mile for the first 10,000 business miles in the tax year and then 25p after that.

7.2.7. Legal and professional costs

Tax avoidance

Claim all the legal and professional fees you incur in the day-to-day running of your rental business (e.g. accountancy fees in preparing the letting business accounts and rental tax liability). Add the legal fees you incur with regard to capital expenditure, e.g. buying or selling the property, to the cost of those transactions.

7.2.8. Spouse as property manager

Tax avoidance

Pay your spouse or partner a wage for dealing with the administration of the let properties, as long as they don't own part of the property. In fact, this is a good way for them to receive some of the income from the property without you having to give them a share in it. Their duties would include finding tenants, arranging inventories, check ins/outs, dealing with tenant queries, keeping rental records, etc.

TIP

Look at what a managing agent would charge you and discount this by 50% for a non specialist putting the hours in. However, you can't pay less than the National Minimum Wage, currently £5.73 per hour. Include these costs under "Legal, management fees for on-going costs of letting".

7.2.9. Split the rental income

Tax avoidance

If one taxpayer pays a higher rate of tax on their income while another does not have enough income to even use up their personal allowance and basic rate tax band, rental income could be split between partners (whether it's your spouse, partner, relative or friend) to avoid tax, by switching the ownership of the property.

For this to be effective the asset must be transferred absolutely and unconditionally.

- in most cases, transferring ownership of the property would generally have its main effect on the income of future years

- transferring assets where the couple is not married or in a civil partnership can result in a Capital Gains Tax (CGT) liability and a potential future Inheritance Tax (IHT) liability

- transfers of assets between partners who are married or are civil partners are free of CGT and could save on CGT when assets are sold if one partner has an unused annual exemption or capital losses.

If you decide to transfer a property to your spouse (or anyone else for that matter), then you will need to let your solicitor know what type of joint ownership you want.

7.3. FURNISHED HOLIDAY HOMES

Letting property is treated as a business; however, it is not treated as a "trade". This means that your net rental income is not considered "earned" income. But there is an exception. If you invest in and let UK property that qualifies as a furnished holiday home, then it will be treated as earned income and will therefore benefit from some attractive income tax rules:

- your net income from holiday lets counts as part of your earnings for pension contributions

- you can claim capital allowances on any money spent on furnishings and equipment for the holiday home

- if you make a loss on your holiday let(s), you can offset it against your other income for the year and claim a tax rebate. There is no relief against general income from any other kind of letting.

With such appealing tax advantages on offer, you won't be surprised to learn that there are strict qualifying criteria, e.g. that the property is actually available for at least 140 days (20 weeks) a year and is let for at least 70 days (ten weeks) a year.

Tɪᴘ

Make sure you keep a booking diary showing the names and addresses of the holidaymakers together with the dates of their stay. This will provide proof to the Taxman if required.

You aren't expected to make a profit on your holiday home each year. But the Taxman would expect to see the holiday home business being profitable over, say, a five-year period. The Taxman may disallow a property as a holiday home even though you fulfil the criteria if your main motive is just to buy a second home (say, for retirement) rather than to run a business at a profit.

Tax avoidance

If you do make a loss, e.g. rental income less than annual mortgage interest, on your holiday let one year, offset it against your other income either in the tax year of the loss or the year before. Compare the tax rates of your income in both years and offset the loss against the year in which you will get the maximum rebate.

Example

Sharon has a furnished holiday property and in the tax year to April 5 2010 she has made a loss of £1,200. Her other income for the year from her employment is £23,000. Sharon can offset the £1,200 loss against her employment income. As she's already paid basic rate tax on her employment income she will receive a tax rebate of £240 (£1,200 x 20%).

In the tax year to April 5 2009 Sharon had employment income of £55,000. Instead of offsetting the loss against her other income in 2009/10, she decided to claim it against her 2008/9 income. In this case she will receive a tax rebate of £480 (£1,200 x 40%) because she was a higher rate taxpayer.

How do you make a claim to deduct the loss from the previous year's income? Either complete Box 17 on page one of the "UK property" pages for a tax return or write to the Taxman.

7.4. RUNNING YOUR OWN BUSINESS

During this phase of your life you might decide to start/run your own business. Strictly, there is no separate "business tax" to avoid. The tax you pay on your business profits depends on the format in which you carry on your business. The right format for you depends on your circumstances. Basically, the choices are limited company, partnership and sole trader.

7.4.1. Limited company

This means that the company is the actual owner of the business. The ownership of the company depends on who owns the shares. It is possible to have just one shareholder, but this is not recommended. Shareholdings in the company are a good way to pass on ownership of the company, say, to the next generation of your family. The company has a separate legal existence to its shareholders and is a method of protecting them - their liability is limited to the money they put into the business. A limited company must also have at least one director and one secretary. Again, it is recommended that there are always at least two directors.

Limited companies are liable to Corporation Tax (CT). This is charged at the following rates; up to 300,000 21% and above £1,500,000 30%. In the gaps between £300,001 and £1,500,000, sliding scales operate to gradually increase rates to the next band.

Tax avoidance

For example, profits have to be extracted from a company. Whilst salaries and bonuses attract NI contributions, dividends do not. However, excessive dividends can push you into higher rates of income tax. The most tax efficient solution will always depend on your particular facts.

7.4.2. Going into partnership

This consists of two or more people carrying on a business together. The terms of their partnership are governed by a partnership agreement. Each partner is charged to tax and class 4 NI on their share of partnership profits for each tax year.

Tax avoidance

For example, you can be flexible about the way in which profits are shared between the partners and this can produce savings on the total tax bill. It is often useful to do this when spouses are carrying out a business together.

7.4.3. Keeping it simple as a sole trader

This is the simplest form of carrying out a business. You are charged to income tax and Class 4 NI on your business profits, each year. Despite anti-avoidance legislation to counteract manipulation of profit periods, there remain considerable opportunities to defer tax by choosing a suitable accounting date.

For 2009/10 the self-employed are liable for class 2 contributions at £2.40 a week, which confers some state benefits. They are also liable to pay class 4 NI at the rate of 8% on profits between £5,715 and £43,875 and at 1% on profits above

£43,875. Class 4 NI buys no state benefits whatsoever and should be regarded as a tax. Failure to notify HMRC of liability to Class 2 contributions immediately (after April 6 2009) will lead to a penalty being imposed.

Tax avoidance

A person can employ their husband or wife in their business, and pay them a salary. This will use up their personal allowances, but the salary must actually be justified by the work done. The salary must actually be paid and recorded. It cannot simply be an entry in your books.

7.4.4. The choice is yours

Do you have complete freedom to choose how your business trades? Yes, the choice is yours. There may be decision points in your business career when you have to think hard about it. For instance, you might be a sole trader, and employing your wife or children. The time comes when you have to think about taking them into partnership. There may also be external pressures. In some industries, for example, people who can award you a contract may refuse to do so unless you are a limited company.

The decision on whether to employ your spouse or be in partnership with him or her is one which depends on various circumstances - many of which are probably nothing to do with saving tax. However, all other things being equal, it is usually better and more flexible to be in partnership.

7.5. IF YOU DECIDE TO GO LIMITED

7.5.1. Transferring an existing business

If you are thinking about making an existing business into a limited company, you need to consider the actual transfer. The limited company must buy the assets from you the existing trader. This could give rise to a CGT liability.

Tax avoidance

However, if the transfer is handled correctly, this can be deferred. The solution is to issue shares in the new company in consideration for the asset of the business bought. This effectively defers the CGT liability until the shares are eventually sold - by that time you may well qualify for entrepreneurs' relief from CGT.

There are three conditions which must be met:

1. The whole of the assets of the business must be transferred to the company.

2. The business must be transferred as a going concern.

3. The business must be transferred wholly or partly in exchange for shares issued by the company to the person(s) transferring the business.

Warning. When transferring a business to a limited company, remember that stamp duty is payable on the value of certain assets such as land, goodwill, debtors, etc.

Trap. If you transfer your business to a limited company which you control, HMRC considers this as a transaction between connected persons. They will then seek to impose a market value on all trading stock which is transferred to the company. This will have the effect of making you taxable on the full selling price of trading stock before you have actually sold it. This could be especially costly where there is a large difference between the cost of trading stock and the full selling price.

Tax avoidance

However, you can make an election for the trading stock to be transferred at the higher of original cost of the amount paid by the company.

7.5.2. Buying an existing business

What if you bought an existing business instead? If you are thinking of doing this, it is important to differentiate between:

- buying a business as a going concern
- buying the assets of a business; and
- buying the shares in a company which is carrying on in a business.

7.5.3. Profit extraction

With a limited company you don't have the same flexibility as sole traders and partnerships in taking money out of the business. If you want to benefit from the profits of the business personally, you have to draw money out. The two chief ways of doing this are paying a salary or a tax-efficient dividend from the company on your shares.

Other methods of profit extraction include:

- charging your company a significant rate of interest on loans you make to it
- renting property you own to your company for its use
- taking a cheap/interest-free loan from your company
- having a company car or letting the company pay for business mileage in your own vehicle
- getting the company to make pension contributions to your personal pension
- use of other company assets rather than buying them yourself

- letting the company provide you with free accommodation

- receiving childcare vouchers from your company

- having your medical cover paid for by your company

- making other members of your family shareholders so that they receive income each time the company pays a dividend

- employing members of your family to work for the company and paying them a tax-efficient salary

- selling personal assets to your company

- charging your company a royalty or licence fee for using one of your inventions/ ideas.

Tax avoidance

However, which is the most tax effective way to get money out of your company? You'll need to choose the one (or combination of several) that best suits your personal circumstances. For each method you are interested in get your advisor to tell you (in simple language) what's involved, the tax consequences for you and your company and whether there are any VAT implications. A worked example wouldn't go amiss too, as would the pros and cons of using that method.

Armed with this information you will be able to devise a simple strategy to withdraw profit and pay the right amount of tax. Focusing on profit extraction won't result in a zero tax bill every time - but it certainly will lead to considerably more of your profit staying in your pocket.

7.5.4. Don't forget the VAT

It is not compulsory for a business to register for VAT unless either its turnover in the preceding twelve months exceeds the registration threshold, or expected turnover in the next month exceeds the threshold. It is possible to register voluntarily before reaching the threshold. Many small businesses delay registration for as long as possible because of the additional administration and fear of a control visit from the VATman. Businesses whose customers cannot recover input VAT would be well advised to delay registration for as long as possible. The input VAT that can be recovered may well exceed the costs of setting up a quarterly reporting system. Input tax recovered in the first six months preceding VAT registration is recoverable.

Look at the timing of receipts and payments. Many small businesses benefit from the cash accounting scheme. This permits you to account for VAT on the basis of receipts and payments during the VAT period, thus giving you automatic relief for slow or bad debtors.

Tax avoidance

Voluntarily register for VAT if you can recover enough input VAT to make it worth-while. Use the right scheme for you. Seek advice on maximising your cash flow/recovery of input VAT by using, say, the cash accounting or flat rate scheme.

7.6. TAX-EFFICIENT INVESTMENTS

Some investments have built-in tax avoidance qualities. The government, usually for policy reasons, has provided an exemption from one or more of the taxes. Other investments are attractive because they fall within a category of asset which is favoured by the tax code. Every investment produces return and every investment has a cost. Investment efficiency is to look at the return on the sum expended, after deductions of all costs. Taxation is one such cost for the individual investor.

7.6.1. What is a tax-efficient investment?

This depends on your particular circumstances:

- an exemption from CGT has no relevance if you can confidently expect to have the full annual exempt amount unused each year

- income tax relief is no good to the non-taxpayer, yet thousands of non-taxpayers hold exempt National Savings products

- every so-called tax-efficient investment must be judged against other action available to you

- it may well be, for you, that paying off (either in whole or in part) the mortgage on your home, on which there is no tax relief, produces a higher effective return than an investment in an ISA

- having said all this there are some investments that have both income tax and CGT advantages.

7.6.2. Individual Savings Accounts (ISAs)

- individuals can invest in two ISAs in any tax year: one cash ISA and one stocks and shares ISA

- 16 and 17-year-olds can contribute to a cash ISA

- however, if a parent provides funds for a child's ISA, the income from that ISA will be taxed on the parent if it exceeds £100 a year

- there is no restriction on grandparents or other relatives providing funds for a child's ISA

- withdrawals from an ISA do not affect the investment limit for the tax year. Once the maximum has been invested, no more investments can be made that year even if the funds have been withdrawn

- money can be transferred between ISAs without affecting the investment limits for the year, subject to some conditions. A cash ISA can be transferred into another cash ISA or into a stocks and shares ISA, but a stocks and shares ISA cannot be transferred into a cash ISA.

7.6.3. Enterprise investment scheme (EIS)

- the EIS gives tax relief for new shares in certain trading companies that are not listed on the Stock Exchange

- income tax relief is given at 20% on sums of up to £500,000 invested in a tax year

- gains on this investment escape CGT after three years

- it is possible to defer CGT on a gain of any size by reinvesting in shares that qualify under the EIS

- the gain must be reinvested in the period between one year before and three years after the disposal

- tax is payable on the deferred gain when the EIS shares are disposed of

- an individual can obtain CGT deferral, but not income tax relief, by reinvesting in a company in which he or she is a director, although there are some restrictions

- this can help people setting up a new business.

7.6.4. Venture capital trusts (VCTs)

- individuals can get income tax relief of 30% on investments of up to £200,000 a year in shares in VCTs in the tax year 2008/09. VCTs resemble investment trusts and invest in a range of companies

- there is no CGT on the sale of these shares and dividends are free of higher rate tax, but the 10% tax credit cannot be recovered

- shares issued after April 5 2006 must be held for five years

- CGT deferral is not available

- EIS and VCT investments carry a high risk and EIS investments may be difficult to realise. While VCTs are more easily realisable, the spread between offer and bid prices can exceed 10%.

7.6.5. Other investments

In addition to investments discussed in this chapter the following may, depending on your circumstances, provide tax advantages:

- an approved pension scheme, whether an employer scheme or a personal pension plan

- unquoted shares providing 100% IHT business property relief (BPR)

- investment in your own business to provide 100% IHT BPR

- investment in a private house to provide a tax-free gain on sale

- subscription by employees for shares under Enterprise Management Incentives

- purchase of government stock or qualifying corporate bonds, providing the possibility of a capital gain that is exempt from CGT at sale.

7.7. TURNING INCOME INTO GAINS

If you could realise a capital gain instead of having taxable income, you could save tax at 22% (18% versus 40%). Indeed, if you use your annual tax-free Capital Gains Tax (CGT) exemption (currently £10,100) you could save the tax altogether.

Example

If you are already a higher rate taxpayer and you expect to make an extra £30,000 profit this year, income tax on this would amount to £12,000 (£30,000 x 40%). However, if you could convert this profit to a capital gain, the CGT at 18% on a £30,000 gain is only £5,400.

Tax avoidance

To receive capital instead of income choose investments (such as some unit trusts) which specialise in capital growth rather than distributing income.

7.7.1. New shares instead of a dividend

If you invest in shares in plcs, you may well, from time to time, receive proposals to issue new shares instead of paying a cash dividend. This is just the sort of bumph which you might usually consign directly to the wastepaper bin.

Instead of a dividend income amount, the plc could be offering you the choice of receiving shares, which you then sell to obtain a capital sum. If the profit (sale proceeds - cost) you make from this eventual sale is within your annual CGT-free allowance (currently £10,100), then you've converted otherwise taxable income into a tax-free gain.

If your advisor is in the habit of picking up dividend details from bank statements he might miss the issue of shares, particularly if the plc's first dividend this year is the same as or comparable to last year.

Tax avoidance

Do not be too hasty in binning bumph from any quoted companies you invest in. Instead of a dividend income, they could be offering shares which you later sell for a tax-free capital sum.

7.7.2. Selling shares "cum dividend"

Offshore funds are open-ended investment funds investing in equities or foreign government stocks. They are resident outside the UK, usually in a recognised tax haven, and are structured either as investment companies or unit trusts. Depending on their tax status under UK law, such funds can have an advantage over their onshore counterparts.

When a share is said to be "cum dividend", it means that it is offered for sale with an entitlement to the next dividend payment attached. This dividend will already have been declared (but not paid) by the company, so the market knows how much it is worth and the share price will reflect this.

Tax avoidance

The advantage of an offshore fund is that it accrues income gross. So sell your investment cum dividend in order to turn income into gains and tax-free by utilising your annual CGT allowance. UK funds accrue their income net of tax which cannot be reclaimed if they are sold cum dividend.

Where can you get one? Minimum investment varies from £100 to £25,000 and investment may be made direct via a fund manager, stockbroker or other intermediary. There are initial and annual management charges, some of which are less transparent than onshore funds.

Warning. There are some disadvantages to these offshore funds which you'll need to weigh against the tax benefits. For example, you might incur exchange gains and losses on the conversion of funds out of and back into Sterling. And investor protection comparable to UK standards may not be available.

7.7.3. Roll up funds

The interest you earn on your savings is taxed as it is credited to your UK (onshore) deposit account. This is either paid to you or added to the account. With the offshore roll up fund you have the following advantages over an onshore deposit (if you are a UK resident taxpayer): **(1)** the account will grow much faster because income is paid gross (no tax deducted) and because of the compound interest effect (i.e. interest on interest); **(2)** tax is only due when the funds are realised.

You can make regular withdrawals of up to 5% of the original investment each year (ending on the anniversary of the policy) without an immediate tax charge. Such withdrawals are treated as partial surrenders and only taken into account in calculating the final profit on the bond when it is cashed in. If this facility is not used in one year, it can be accumulated for use later, which is especially useful if you want to save this for a particularly costly item of expenditure.

Tax avoidance

Your investment shields (rolls up) returns from tax, or at least until the investment is cashed in. Obviously, if you cash the bond in too early, the charges incurred might exceed the investment returns.

7.7.4. Gain on incorporation

If you are running your business as a sole trader or a partnership, you can transfer all the assets and liabilities of that business to a company tax-free. If the business is profitable, any capital gain you make on this transfer is rolled over until you sell the shares in the company, provided the only consideration you receive is shares in that company.

Let's say that, after incorporation, the trading company makes profits which you wish to draw out. You can do this by taking a dividend on these shares but you will be liable to income tax rates on this.

Tax avoidance

Sell an unincorporated business to a company in exchange for ordinary and redeemable shares. In due course, as the company makes profits, it could redeem your preference shares rather than pay you a dividend. The tax rate on this could be only 18%. Redeem some of your preference shares to crystallise some of the gain you rolled over on incorporation.

> **TIP**
>
> To redeem the shares, you need to hold a board meeting to record your decision, give the shareholders notice of what you intend to do and finally file a record of the redemption at Companies House (Form 122). A company formation agent can draft the articles and provide the documentation you need.

Warning. Don't try to do this too quickly or turn ordinary shares into redeemable shares just to use this tactic. If you do, the Taxman will argue the capital gain should be treated as a dividend, meaning more tax to pay.

7.8. PENSION CONTRIBUTIONS

Most contributions to registered personal pensions made by an individual are paid net of basic rate tax. Deducting basic rate tax has the effect of automatically giving you basic rate tax relief. The pension company reclaims the 20% tax from HMRC. For example, a person paying £3,600 into a pension will actually pay the pension company £2,880 (£3,600 less basic rate tax of 20%).

If you pay higher rate tax on any of your income, you are entitled to higher rate tax relief on personal pension payments.

7.8.1. How much can you contribute?

There is an annual and a lifetime limit on the pension contributions you can make. An annual contribution has been set at £245,000 for 2009/10 increasing to £255,000 in 2010/11. If you exceed this, you will be taxed personally on the excess at 40%.

There is also a lifetime limit of £1.75 million (for 2009/10) on the pension value attracting relief. This will increase to £1.8 million for 2010/11 and thereafter will be reviewed at five-yearly intervals. Any excess is subject to a recovery charge when you draw benefits from the fund. You'd pay tax at 25% on the excess funds used to create a pension and 40% on those taken as a lump sum.

Tax avoidance

Because of the high limits on pension contributions, it is no longer necessary to maximise payments each year. However, making pension payments up to the amount of your income subject to higher rate tax in any tax year will maximise the tax you can avoid.

7.9. GIFT AID

Tax relief is available on donations to charity under Gift Aid. Tax relief at the basic and higher rates is given in the same way as for personal pension contributions.

However, unlike pension contributions you can elect to have your donation treated as if it were paid in the previous year.

The tax-efficiency of this form of giving is so obvious that there have been frequent attempts at abuse. At least one taxpayer has been investigated for simply putting a figure (of, say, £10,000) for Gift Aid payments on their tax return, which turned out to be unsubstantiated.

Example

Anne is a higher rate taxpayer. She makes a Gift Aid payment of £1,000 in 2008/9. Her tax position is as follows:

	£
Payment made to charity	1,000
20% treated as deducted by taxpayer (paid to the charity by HMRC)	250
Total received by charity	1,250
Tax relief at 40%	500
Net cost to Anne	750

If Anne wishes to pass on the benefit of the higher rate relief to the charity, she should make a payment of £1,300. The total received by the charity would be £1,625 (1,300 x 100/80, i.e. 100-20) Anne would receive tax relief of £650 (£1,625 x 40%), leaving a net cost to her of £1,000.

If Anne is an employee and pays all her tax through the PAYE system, the higher rate relief could be given by a coding adjustment. Otherwise, she would need to claim relief through the self-assessment return.

7.10. GIFTS AND INHERITANCE TAX (IHT)

IHT is payable if the sum of a person's assets at death and the gifts they made in the seven years before death exceed £325,000, subject to various reliefs and exemptions. However, there are lots of gifts and transfers you can make each year, which enable you to avoid IHT altogether. These are as follows:

7.10.1. £3,000 annual exemption

Each individual may give £3,000 away every year without any IHT consequence at all. If you did not use this last year, then you may carry it forward and give away £6,000 this year. So a husband and wife can give £12,000 away, thus saving £4,800 (£12,000 x 40%) in potential tax without any difficulty at all.

7.10.2. £250 gifts

Gifts of up to £250 may be given to anybody. They are unlimited and you could, theoretically give £250 to every teacher in your child's school. But if you give £251 away, the whole £251 will be taxable and not just the odd £1.

7.10.3. Gifts on marriage

You are able to make gifts to one of the partners of a marriage or their children. The limits are £5,000 if the donor is a parent of one of the individuals getting married, or £2,500 if the donor is a grandparent or great-grandparent. Otherwise, the limit for tax-free gifts is £1,000.

7.10.4. Normal expenditure out of income

You can give away almost any amount as long as it is seen to be normal expenditure from your income, is not manifestly from capital, and is capable of being repeated year on year. So if you are retired with a fantastic index-linked pension of, say, £50,000 p.a. and only spend £10,000 a year, you could theoretically give the rest away as normal expenditure without IHT consequences.

7.10.5. The seven-year rule and taper relief

If you make a gift, which is known as a Potentially Exempt Transfer (PET), as long as you live seven years, it will be completely free of tax. However, if you die within the seven-year period, it will fall into charge with the rest of your chargeable estate. Fortunately, there is taper relief. So if you die between years three and seven, the tax payable will be reduced by 20% increments down to zero. So it makes sense to make gifts as soon as you can in order to get the seven-year clock running.

7.10.6. No gifts with reservation

The Taxman isn't stupid and won't let you "give things away" but keep them. For example, if you have a collection of old masters, and you simply say to your children "right, this lot is yours", and leave them on your walls the gift will not count. The old masters will still be part of your estate. It's also no use passing over £50,000 into a building society account in your children's names, but having the cheque book and cash card for it.

TIP
When you give something away, exclude yourself from continuing to benefit from it.

7

Maximising income

Rental income

1. As you can't get relief on a loan to buy your own property, aim to borrow as much as possible (with interest-only loans) against your investment properties and use the rental profits to pay off the mortgage on your own property. That way you will get tax relief on all your borrowings.

2. The wear and tear allowance will usually work out to be more beneficial than claiming the actual cost of replacement furniture.

3. Rental income could be split between partners (whether it's your spouse, partner, relative or friend), to avoid tax, by sharing the ownership of the property.

Running your own business

1. Profits have to be extracted from a company. Whilst salaries and bonuses attract NI contributions, dividends do not. However, excessive dividends can push you into higher rates of income tax. The most tax-efficient solution will always depend on your particular circumstances.

2. You can employ your partner in your business and pay them a salary. This will use up their personal allowances, but the salary must actually be justified by the work done.

Turning income into gains

1. If you could realise a capital gain instead of having taxable income, you could save tax at 22% (18% versus 40%). Indeed, if you use your annual tax-free Capital Gains Tax (CGT) exemption (currently £10,100), you could save the tax altogether.

2. To receive capital instead of income choose investments (such as some unit trusts) which specialise in capital growth rather than distributing income.

3. Do not be too hasty in binning bumph from any quoted companies you invest in. Instead of a dividend income they could be offering shares which you later sell for a tax-free capital sum.

KEY POINTS

Pensions

1. Most contributions to registered personal pensions made by an individual are paid net of basic rate tax. Deducting basic rate tax has the effect of automatically giving you basic rate tax relief.

2. If you pay higher rate tax on any of your income, you are entitled to higher rate tax relief on personal pension payments but you have to claim it.

3. Because of the high limits for tax relief on pension contributions, it's no longer necessary to maximise your payments each tax year. However, making pension payments up to the amount of your income subject to higher rate tax in any tax year will maximise the tax you can avoid.

Gift Aid

1. Tax relief is available on donations to charity under Gift Aid. Any donation to a charity established in the UK will qualify if you make a declaration.

2. If you are a higher rate taxpayer in 2009/10 but weren't in 2008/9, elect for donations made in 2009/10 to be treated for tax purposes as if they had been made in 2008/9.

Gifts and Inheritance Tax (IHT)

1. IHT is payable if the sum of your assets at death and the gifts you made in the seven years before death exceed £325,000.

2. You can give £3,000 away every year without any IHT consequence at all. If you did not use this last year, then you may carry it forward and give away £6,000 this year. So a husband and wife can give £12,000 away, thus saving £4,800.

3. You can give away almost any amount as long as it is seen to be normal expenditure from your income, and is capable of being repeated year on year.

CHAPTER 8

Providing for retirement

8.1. INTRODUCTION

Your objective in planning for retirement is likely to be to achieve maximum capital accumulation. Indeed, there may come a time, say, with children off your hands and mortgages repaid, you will be in a strong position to add to pension funds or to establish investment portfolios.

However, pension planning is an important part of any annual tax avoidance planning (for those aged under 75) because contributions to registered pension schemes qualify for tax relief at the individual's highest rate. The key question is how much can you contribute each year and still avoid tax?

The pension funds you are paying into have always enjoyed many tax avoidance benefits, including the ability to receive investment income and enjoy capital growth in a tax-free environment. These funds are generally inaccessible until you reach age 55 (50 until April 5 2010). However, when the pension benefits are taken, you can have up to a quarter of the fund in cash tax-free, while the pension for the rest of your life is taxable. There are even some tax avoidance strategies using this 25% tax-free bonus more than once.

Another part of your retirement plan might be passing on or selling your business. The good news is that the current capital tax regime is probably as favourable as it is ever going to be in terms of providing for succession in, or the selling of, the family or owner-managed company. For example, all shareholdings in unquoted trading companies are completely exempt from Inheritance Tax (IHT) and you can plan to improve your chance of getting entrepreneurs' relief on the sale of your business.

8.2. PENSION CONTRIBUTIONS

Most contributions to registered personal pensions made by an individual are paid net of basic rate tax. Deducting basic rate tax has the effect of automatically giving you basic rate tax relief. You do not have to claim this tax relief from HMRC, the pension company reclaims the 20% tax from HMRC. For example, a person paying £3,600 into a pension will actually pay the pension company £2,880 (£3,600 less basic rate tax of 20%).

If you pay higher rate tax on any of your income, you are entitled to higher rate tax relief on personal pension payments.

8.2.1. How much can you put away tax-free?

Annual contribution

This has been set at £245,000 for 2009/10 increasing to £255,000 in 2010/11. If you exceed this, you will be taxed personally on the excess at 40%.

Lifetime limit

There is also a limit of £1.75 million (for 2009/10) on the pension value attracting relief. This will increase to £1.8 million for 2010/11 and thereafter will be reviewed at five-yearly intervals. Any excess is subject to a recovery charge when you draw benefits from the fund. You'd pay tax at 25% on the excess funds used to create a pension and 40% on those taken as a lump sum.

Your tax relief

Tax relief for contributions to a registered pension scheme are generous in that income tax relief is given on the greater of £3,600 (gross or 100% of your taxable earnings). Your taxable earnings broadly include employment income and benefits - dividends and investment income are not included.

Yes, your tax relief is limited to the annual allowance, but there is no pension earnings cap. This gives considerably more flexibility for you as a high earner. Because of the high limits on pension contributions, it is no longer necessary for most individuals to maximise payments each year.

Making pension payments up to the amount of income subject to higher rate tax will maximise the benefit. Where pension payments are paid net of tax at 20%, it is the grossed up payment that should not exceed the income subject to higher rate tax where possible.

It is possible to set up a personal pension for a partner with little or no earnings or even children so they can benefit from tax relief at 20%, even if they do not actually pay any tax.

Tax avoidance

Because of the high limits on pension contributions, it is no longer necessary to maximise payments each year. However, making pension payments up to the amount of your income subject to higher rate tax in any tax year will maximise the tax you can avoid.

8.2.2. Contracting out of S2P

An employee who is not a member of a contracted-out pension scheme can contract out of the State Second Pension (S2P) using a personal pension. The employee and employer continue to pay full NI but part of the payment is transferred to the employee's personal pension plan.

TIP

Anyone who wants to contract out of S2P for the current year should do so before April 6 2010.

This is also the date by which contracted-out individuals can contract back into S2P for the current tax year. Several insurance companies and financial advisors consider that at present the balance is usually in favour of being contracted into S2P. However, the argument could soon become academic, because contracting out via a personal pension is likely to end after 2011/12.

8.2.3. Non-cash contributions

If you make a cash contribution to a registered pension scheme, both you and the pension fund get a tax break.

Example 1 - cash

Simon says he will earn £150,000 in 2009/10. So he could make a contribution into his pension scheme up to £150,000 (100% of his earnings). To fund his contribution this year he sells his share portfolio (which unfortunately has crashed from £160,000 to £120,000). The cash effect for Simon and his pension scheme is as follows:

	£
Pension fund receives:	
Net contribution from Simon	120,000
Tax reclaimed by fund managers	30,000
Total received by fund	**150,000**
Simon receives:	
Tax-free cash draw-down	37,500
Tax relief at 20%	24,000
Total cash received	**61,500**
Less loss on share sales	(40,000)
Simon's net cash position	**21,500**

However, you don't actually need cash to make a pension contribution, as you can treat a transfer of an asset into a pension fund as a contribution and still get tax relief.

Example 2 - non cash

Robin is in the same position as Simon but he optimistically believes the stock market will recover, so he doesn't want to sell his share portfolio. However, he also needs to boost the value of his pension fund as he wants to retire in ten years' time. Robin decides to transfer his shares directly into his Self-Invested Pension Plan (SIPP).

Robin's cash position is almost the same as Simon's because the transfer of his shares to the SIPP is treated as a sale for tax purposes. The difference is that the pension trustees must pay Stamp Duty of £750 (0.5% x £150,000) on the acquisition of the shares, which will reduce the fund value slightly.

Robin can make a transfer of his shares directly to his pension scheme as it's a self-invested scheme, which means he has some control over what it invests in. This would not be possible with a standard personal pension scheme.

Once the shares are inside the SIPP, any increase in their value is protected from Capital Gains Tax. Robin has also retained control over his share portfolio and he will continue to benefit from its growth in value.

The value of many assets has fallen in the economic downturn. While that is generally bad news, it is most probably temporary, and shares and property are likely to appreciate again in the future. Until then, the depressed values present an opportunity to make gifts or to carry out other transactions that you might have considered before but put off because of the tax implications. Often the tax arising from a transaction is related to the value of the asset, so the lower the value the less tax to pay.

Tax avoidance

If you have a SIPP you could take advantage of the current low value of the stock market by transferring quoted shares you own into your fund as a pension contribution. Where the shares are standing at a loss, you pay no tax on the transfer, and you get full tax relief on the value contributed to the scheme. Any future increase in value will be protected from tax within your pension scheme.

TIP

Open market assets such as quoted shares should be accepted without valuation as a transfer in specie by the pension fund trustees.

TIP

You can transfer a wide range of assets into a SIPP, including unquoted shares and non-residential property.

Tax avoidance

If you transfer assets to your SIPP while their values are depressed, you could pay little or no Capital Gains Tax and future growth will be tax-free. You will also receive tax relief on the value transferred.

8.2.4. Employer's contribution

You may normally pay a regular portion of your salary, or a lump sum, into a pension scheme. Your employer can pay this pension contribution on your behalf.

The employer could pay the pension contribution directly to the pension company giving the reference number of your scheme. A pension contribution paid this way is treated as a gross contribution, meaning there's no additional tax rebate if you're a 40% taxpayer.

However, any contribution paid by your company into your pension scheme must be deducted from the maximum contributions you are permitted to pay for that tax year.

Tax avoidance

A pension contribution made by your company is not taxable on you. When you eventually receive a pension from the pension scheme that will be taxed. However, this may well be a time when you are only a 20% taxpayer rather than taxed at higher rates, so you'd gain that way.

Tax avoidance

The company can pay a pension contribution on behalf of your spouse or other relatives into a stakeholder pension scheme set up in their name, as long as the maximum contribution limit is not exceeded for each individual. The contributions paid for individuals who are not employees of the company will not be tax-deductible, but the individuals for whom the contributions are paid will not be taxed on them.

Tax avoidance

The pension contribution is tax-deductible for your employer provided the Taxman doesn't think it's excessive. One way to justify a larger pension contribution than normal is to establish that it is for past service, when your employer did not have a pension scheme.

As the pension contribution is not paid directly to you, there is no effect on your personal tax position. However, if the pension contribution paid by your employer replaces a contribution you would normally pay out of your net salary, you will be left with more money to spend.

8.2.5. New regulations

The Chancellor announced that relief for pension contributions is to be restricted as from April 6 2011. This restriction, though unwelcome, will be easy to follow and is consistent with the introduction of the 50% top rate of income tax in 2010/11. However, provisions intended to penalise anyone who makes extra contributions before the new rules come into effect (anti-forestalling), which apply between April 22 2009 and April 5 2011, threaten to penalise innocent contributors to pension schemes.

Trap. If you scale back your pension contributions in 2009/10, you are reducing what can be classed as regular contributions and so avoid the forestalling provisions between now and 2011.

8.2.6. Trivial pension funds

Once you're over the retirement age for your pension scheme you can draw 25% of the fund as a tax-free lump sum. Your scheme's retirement age could be as low as 50 if you were born before April 6 1960. Those younger need to reach at least 55 before drawing a tax-free lump sum. When the time comes you can take 25% of your pension fund as an immediate cash payment. The balance must be used to provide a pension for the rest of your life. Although the pension rules are now more flexible, ultimately you'll probably have to use some of your fund to buy an annuity.

However, there's an exception to this general rule. Funds which have a value of £18,000 or less can be fully withdrawn in cash. You may not think this could help you but with some lateral thinking there could be a way for you to take advantage.

The pension schemes legislation includes special rules that apply to funds worth less than £18,000. These are officially referred to as "trivial funds", and you're allowed to draw out the fund in full provided that:

- you're aged between 60 and 75

- the value of all your pension funds added together is no more than £18,000 (see note)

- if you have more than one fund, you must cash them all in within a twelve-month period

- 25% of the fund(s) value can be taken tax-free, the balance will be taxed at the basic rate

- the pension company will allow you to do it.

Note. The trivial limit is worked out by taking 1% of the pension's "lifetime allowance" figure when you retire.

Example - non-worker

Fred has paid into a pension fund for himself but not for his wife. He plans to retire in a few years' time when his wife reaches 60. Her only income is from investments and she pays basic rate tax. Fred decides to start paying £200 per month into a personal pension for her. The Taxman will add £50 tax relief per month directly into the fund. After five years Fred's contributions will add up to £12,000. Adding on the tax relief and assuming an annual growth rate, net of pension scheme charges, of around 3.25% there could be around £16,500 in the fund. That's a pretty good return thanks to help from the Taxman.

Even if you have no earned income, and don't pay any tax, you're allowed to pay up to £2,880 net each year into a personal pension scheme. The Taxman will add a further £720 as a tax incentive.

Example - worker

Fred's wife plans to retire in March 2011 when she reaches 60. The Taxman's rules say that you can pay personal pension premiums up to the level of your gross annual earnings. So Fred employs his wife starting in September 2009. He pays her a salary of £18,000 per year. In February 2011 he sets up a pension scheme for her and pays a premium of £14,400 into it. The Taxman adds a further £3,600. In April 2011 the fund, after charges, should be worth around £17,700. Fred's wife can draw £4,425 tax-free, and the balance net of basic rate tax will be £10,620. So in the space of two months Fred's wife has gained £645 courtesy of the Taxman.

TIP

If there's more than one pension fund within the £18,000 limit, cashing them in over two tax years could reduce the tax payable.

Tax avoidance

If you or your spouse's pension fund has a total value of less than £18,000, you can draw it out, in full, all at once. You can draw 25% of its value tax-free. Taking the fund over two tax years could reduce the tax payable on the balance.

8.3. PASSING ON A BUSINESS

8.3.1. Lifetime transfers

If you want to transfer shares in your company to your children or other members of your family, it can be done in one of two ways. Shares could be transferred on a phased basis as you approach retirement. Such transfers will qualify as Partially Exempt Transfers (PET) for IHT and CGT purposes. Business asset holdover relief should normally be available provided neither you nor your spouse can benefit.

The effect of the holdover election is to pass the contingent CGT liability to the new shareholder(s). As the transfer is a PET, if you die within seven years, an IHT charge will arise (subject to the availability of business property relief (BPR)).

8.3.2. Passing shares on death

Since April 1996, 100% BPR has applied to all shareholdings (including non-voting and preference) shares in unquoted trading companies. (Shares in AIM companies are unquoted for this purpose and hence rank for 100% BPR). Unquoted shares are completely exempt from IHT both on lifetime transfers and on death. BPR works by reducing the value transferred, in this case to nil.

To qualify for BPR you need to have held your shareholding for at least two years prior to the transfer/death. BPR is available for both working and passive shareholders, it is not necessary for the shareholder to be a director or work full-time for the company.

You could retain your shares (or most of them) until death. Normally the shares would pass to the children, etc. free of IHT due to the availability of 100% BPR. The children will also inherit the shares at their market value at the date of death for CGT purposes.

Tax avoidance

Consider retaining shares in the family/owner-managed company to obtain complete exemption from IHT on death (donees also inherit shares at market value for CGT). However, lifetime transfers of shares to the next generation (which may be necessary to preserve management morale etc.) are usually tax-free, but the donee takes on a deferred CGT liability.

Tax avoidance

If your family members plan to sell their shares shortly after death, there will be no claw back of BPR and there should be little or no CGT. It will normally be necessary to adjust the probate value of the shares afterwards.

Tax avoidance

If there is a possibility the company may be sold, consider giving away some shares at an early stage to enable your children to maximise their taper relief. This would be a PET, but BPR would only protect the shares from tax on a death in seven years, provided the children had not sold their shares at that stage.

In your will

Adopt a similar strategy in relation to your BPR eligible shares and any other BPR qualifying assets. Do not leave them to your surviving spouse. Leave them directly to your children or through an appropriate discretionary trust (with the surviving spouse being included as one of the beneficiaries).

8.3.3. Avoiding a binding contract

In the event of your death, the other shareholders may have to buy the shares at market value under a "put and call" option arrangement. The other shareholders' obligations to buy your shares could be covered by "shareholders protection insurance" (a policy would be taken out on the life of each shareholder written into trust for the benefit of the others). It is also possible for your shares to be purchased by the company with the company taking out a keyman insurance policy for this purpose.

TIP

Take out a keyman insurance policy to provide a cash sum for the company in the event of your death. The company can then use this money to buy back your shares so as to leave cash for your spouse and other dependants. However, there must be no binding contract to buy back the shares since this would lose you 100% BPR on your shares. A simple call (to buy your shares) option granted to the company should achieve the same result without any loss of BPR.

TIP

Alternatively, nominate (at the discretion of the pension fund trustees) the tax-free "death-in-service" amount of your pension policy in favour of a family discretionary trust (perhaps including your spouse). The sum could then be used to purchase illiquid assets from your estate, such as shares in your company.

Tax avoidance

Set up life assurance arrangements to cover any potential IHT liabilities which cannot be mitigated by planning. The premiums can normally be paid for the benefit of other members of your family free of IHT under the normal expenditure out of income rule or annual £3,000 exemption. The proceeds of the policy are to be held on trust for the beneficiaries so they do not form part of your estate.

8.4. SELLING A BUSINESS

8.4.1. Implications of selling

On the face of it, it would be easy to assume that the only tax you should be concerned with is Capital Gains Tax (CGT) on any profit on disposal. Except in the most straightforward of cases the position is much more complex:

- the tax position and tax losses (if any) of your business may affect the price

- you will be required to give warranties concerning the business and assets of your business

- if offered you may have to decide how much of the sale price you are prepared to leave outstanding on deferred terms

- you will need to consider whether the maximum value is to be achieved by taking the whole of the sale proceeds in capital form and if so an immediate cash sum is the best form of consideration

- the sale of your business may have implications for income tax, Corporation Tax (CT) on company profits and IHT.

8.4.2. Timing

The sale of your business will involve a disposal for CGT purposes. The date of the disposal for CGT will be the point at which you enter into an unconditional contract and not the date of completion. Under self-assessment you are liable to pay your CGT bill on the sale by January 31 following the tax year in which the sale is made.

Tax avoidance

If you are close to a tax year-end, consider deferring the date of disposal until after April 6 (the start of a new tax year) as this will delay the payment of the tax by one year.

8.4.3. Apportionment of sale consideration

The tax payable will depend on the nature of each asset and the consideration that has been attributed to each one. It is important to achieve a sensible allocation of the total price paid for the business amongst the various individual assets and this needs to be specified in the sale agreement.

Provided you and the buyer have negotiated the price at "arm's length" and the allocation has been specified in the sale agreement, the Taxman is unlikely to challenge your apportionment of the total price to individual assets.

Tax avoidance

If your business has unused trading losses which would be lost on cessation, absorb them by allocating higher values to assets that will produce additional trading receipts, such as trading stock, or plant and machinery, which would produce a balancing charge.

Tax avoidance

Place a realistic value on the business' books and records. Keep the value of each individual file, book etc. below the £6,000 CGT chattel exemption. Given the wide range of the underlying books, files and computer records, it's difficult for the Taxman to argue that they are a set. If they were, this would negate the CGT benefit of each individual item being below £6,000.

8.4.4. VAT

VAT may be payable on the sale of assets. The charge to VAT can be avoided on the transfer of the business as a going concern (TOGC). If the transaction is not a TOGC, VAT will be chargeable on taxable assets, e.g. goodwill, stock, plant and machinery and on certain types of commercial land and buildings.

Whether your transaction will qualify as a TOGC depends on the facts and although this is usually agreed between you and the buyer, the VATman is not bound by your decisions.

> **TIP**
>
> Seek to cover your VAT risk with cash or security until confirmation of the VAT position has been obtained. And make sure the contract for sale stipulates that the agreed consideration is exclusive of any VAT which may be payable. Furthermore, have a contractual right included for you to raise a VAT invoice should the VATman subsequently decide that VAT should have been charged on the sale.

8.4.5. Selling shares in a company

You can sell your shares for: **(1)** cash; **(2)** shares in the acquiring company; **(3)** loan notes issued by the acquiring company; and **(4)** a mixture of the above. You may be paid immediately on completion or on a deferred basis. Deferred consideration can either be structured as fixed or variable, e.g. depending on the future profits of a so-called earn-out arrangement. There is much to be said for receiving all of the consideration up front as a guaranteed amount despite the fact that it will attract an immediate tax liability.

8.5. ENTREPRENEURS' RELIEF

8.5.1. 10% not 18% CGT

Both taper relief and indexation allowance were scrapped for all gains made after April 5 2008. This meant small business owners would see a hike in the tax they paid on the sale of their businesses from 10% to 18%.

Tax avoidance

Entrepreneurs' relief (ER) can apply when you sell part or all of your business, or shares in your own company after April 5 2008, subject to a gains cap of £1 million. The capital gain will be reduced to 5/9ths of the full gain, making the effective Capital Gains Tax (CGT) rate 10% (5/9 x 18%). That's if all the right conditions are met of course.

8.5.2. General conditions

You must have held the shares or assets for at least a year before the sale, and the business must be trading, so property letting businesses don't qualify. Where you sell a company, you must own at least 5% of the voting ordinary shares, and have either worked in, or been an officer of, the company or an associated company.

Example

You sell the shares in your company for a gain of £450,000. ER reduces the gain to £250,000 (5/9 x £450,000). The tax due is £45,000 (18% x £250,000); an effective rate of 10% on the full gain of £450,000. You can also deduct your annual exemption (£10,100 for 2009/10), and any capital losses from the taxable gain to reduce your tax bill even further.

There is no minimum age limit on ER, so you don't have to "retire" when you sell your business to qualify. But you do need to consider the £1 million cap that can be subject to the relief. This means you can make a number of gains totalling £1 million over several years, and claim ER on them all. Any gains in excess of £1 million will be taxed at the full 18%.

Example

Gene owned a freehold sports shop and a leasehold shoe shop. He sells the businesses in May 2009 and May 2010 respectively, and makes the following gains and losses:

2009/10	£	£
Sports shop - sold May 2009		
Freehold		520,000
Goodwill		200,000
Net gain		720,000
Entrepreneur's relief 4/9	£720,000	(320,000)
Taxable gain		400,000

2010/11	£	£
Shoe shop - sold May 2010		
Leasehold		(40,000)
Goodwill		400,000
Net gain		360,000
Lifetime limit for entrepreneurs' relief	1,000,000	
Gains used in an ER claim previously	(720,000)	
Available to use against 2010/11 gain	280,000	
Entrepreneurs' relief 4/9 x £280,000		(124,445)
Taxable gain		235,555

Gene's claim for ER is restricted as his total gains, which have been brought into an ER claim, exceeds the lifetime cap of £1million.

However, the Taxman has said that he has no plans to monitor the £1 million limit himself. It will be up to you to keep a record of how much of your lifetime limit you use up over the years.

8.5.3. ER and shares in a company

To qualify for ER the shares being sold must be in the owner's personal company, the definition of which is:

- one in which the shareholder owns at least 5% of the ordinary share capital of the company and, as a result, can exercise 5% of the voting rights; and

- the owner has been an officer or employee for the twelve months prior to the sale.

If the shareholder hasn't been an employee or officer in the company for the twelve months, they won't qualify for ER, so will attract CGT at 18% not 10%. In our example that's extra tax of £36,000.

> **TIP**
>
> Obviously, being a director would qualify as an officer of the company. And just being the company secretary would also help qualify a shareholder for ER. For example, if your spouse also holds shares but doesn't work for the company and isn't already a director, make them company secretary in order for their shareholding to qualify.

> **TIP**
>
> Make sure you have some form of employment relationship with the company. There is no requirement to be a full-time employee of the company, so part-time jobs or consultancy contracts with the company would suffice. Back this up with contracts of employment and by putting yourself on the payroll.

Tax avoidance

Sales of shares are disqualified from ER if the shareholder was not an employee/officer (in the preceding twelve months). So make sure each shareholder is made an employee/officer for that period, e.g. ensure you have a contract.

KEY POINTS

Pension contributions

1. Substantial company pension contributions in respect of directors must be capable of justification (based on the entire reward package, including the contribution).

2. Consider a company pension (self-administered) scheme for directors to be used as a tax-saving vehicle.

3. You can hold up to £1.75 million (rising to £1.8m in 2010/11) in your pension fund on a tax-privileged basis.

4. If you personally own the company's trading property, you can realise cash (usually at a favourable CGT rate) by selling your property at market value to your pension fund. However, this might involve a Stamp Duty Land Tax charge for the pension fund.

5. Consider salary sacrifice arrangements as a means of securing additional pension contributions.

6. Contributions of up to £3,600 per year may be made by an individual to a pension scheme for a non-working shareholder, including spouses, children and grandchildren.

Succession planning

1. Business property relief (BPR) applies to all shareholdings (including non-voting and preference) in unquoted trading companies. These shares are completely exempt from IHT both on lifetime transfers and on death. To qualify for BPR you need to have held your shareholding for at least two years prior to the transfer/death.

2. Consider retaining shares in the family/owner-managed company to obtain complete exemption from IHT on death (donees also inherit shares at market value for CGT.

3. Draft your will to maximise use of BPR and the IHT nil rate band (currently £325,000). In many cases it will be beneficial to leave shares and other assets qualifying for BPR via a discretionary will trust (which could include the surviving spouse as one of the beneficiaries).

4. Take out keyman or shareholders protection insurance to provide a cash sum for your company in the event of your death. It can then use these funds to buy-back your shares on death so as to provide cash for your spouse and other dependants.

Selling your business

1. The sale of your business will involve a disposal for CGT purposes. The date of the disposal for CGT will be the point at which you enter into an unconditional contract and not the date of completion.

2. If you are close to a tax year-end, consider deferring the date of disposal until after April 6 as this will delay the payment of the tax by one year.

3. Place a realistic value on the business' books and records. Keep the value of each individual file, book, etc. below the £6,000 CGT chattel exemption.

4. Entrepreneurs' relief (ER) can apply when you sell part or all of your business, or shares in your own company, subject to a gains cap of £1 million. The capital gain will be reduced to 5/9ths of the full gain, making the effective CGT rate 10% (5/9 x 18%).

5. The Taxman has said that he has no plans to monitor the £1 million limit himself. It will be up to you t keep a record of how much of your lifetime limit you use up over the years.

6. Sales of shares are disqualified from ER if the shareholder was not an employee/officer (in the preceding twelve months). So make sure each shareholder is made an employee/officer for that period, e.g. ensure you have a contract.

CHAPTER 9

Retirement

9.1. INTRODUCTION

Increasing longevity and early retirement ages could mean that you will spend a long time in retirement when you are still physically and mentally active. You might take up a second career, often on a self-employed or consultancy basis or as an executive director of a small company. But how much tax will you actually have to pay on these various sources? In retirement there are a few rough edges to the tax system to be avoided.

9.2. SHOULD YOU BE PAYING TAX AT ALL?

When you reach state pension age (65 years for men and between 60 and 65 years for women, depending on year of birth) you no longer pay NI contributions; however, you don't automatically stop paying income tax. If your taxable income - including your state pension - is more than your tax-free allowances you're still a taxpayer. However, if your tax-free allowances are the same as or more than your taxable income, no action is necessary.

Much depends on the scale and balance of income: how much income there is from each source and how much is taxed at source, for example:

1. If your level of untaxed income, e.g. state pension and self-employed income, is low and your taxed income, e.g. savings and employer's pension, is relatively high, then it may be possible for all the tax you need to pay to be deducted at source.

2. If your untaxed income is high - you might have a SERPs addition to the state pension, or high self-employed earnings - then you will get a tax bill from HMRC.

9.3. INCREASED ALLOWANCES

People aged over 65 are entitled to a larger amount of tax-free income (the personal allowance). However, these allowances are restricted for those on higher incomes. For example, in the tax year that you reach 65, you are entitled to a personal allowance of £9,490; up from £6,475 for those under 65.

At age 75, the personal allowance increases again to £9,640. The Married Couple's Allowance is available only to couples where one partner was born before April 6 1935. (It has been withdrawn for those born in subsequent years.) In 2009/10 it is worth £6,965 if you are 75 or over.

9.3.1. Avoiding the income restriction

If your income is over a certain level, the higher age related tax-free allowance is restricted. For the 2009/10 tax year, the income level is £22,900 per year. The restriction is that your allowance is reduced by one half of the excess of your income over the limit. However, the lowest this can go is to the level of the normal personal allowance for that tax year, which for 2009/10 is £6,475.

Tax avoidance

The marginal tax rate for those over 65 with income over £20,900 can be as high as 33%, so investments that produce tax-free income or capital gains should be considered in those circumstances.

Tax avoidance

In reckoning your income for age allowances, any investment bond withdrawals over the 5% limit have to be taken into account even though there is no tax to pay on the excess at the higher rate. Conversely, the gross amount of a properly recorded donation to a charity reduces your income when calculating whether age allowances are to be restricted. The same applies to personal pension contribution.

Tax avoidance

If your spouse does not have enough income to cover their personal allowance for income tax, you should consider transferring some of your assets to them if practicable, so that the income from them will then be theirs and not yours.

9.3.2. Errors with tax codes

Trap. However, there is more scope for errors. Often, the increased allowances for those over 65 offset the impact of having the state pension - which is taxable, but is not taxed at source.

Example

Lucy is an elderly widow with a state pension and a small annuity. She worked in a part-time job at a supermarket until she was 65. Like the majority of pensioners she was surprised that the state pension is taxable. She was upset to receive a demand for £1,143 for unpaid tax payable immediately, and dismayed to have to deal with a self-assessment tax return for the first time.

Looking at Lucy's payslips this problem could have been anticipated when she first drew her pension. For example in 2009/10 the supermarket earnings had a tax coding of 647L, the "standard" coding for this year. This tells us that full tax-free personal allowance is being allocated to her supermarket employment - leaving nothing to cover the untaxed state pension income.

Unfortunately, as the state pension is taxable, but it is not taxed at source, the tax due on it should have been collected from the supermarket earnings. This is achieved by reducing the tax code to take account of the expected state pension income. Lucy's tax code should have been lower in the year the state pension started. With 30 weeks' pension of £95.25 per week, for example, her code would have fallen from 647L to 361L.

Warning. HMRC rules make it clear that you should take advice if you don't understand your tax coding. The warning is clear: take note or take a risk. So what can you do to reduce coding errors?

9.4. STATE PENSION

The basic state pension from April 2009 is £95.25 per week (single) and £152.30 (couple). This generally increases each year in line with the Retail Prices Index. The starting age is 65 years for men and between 60 and 65 years for women, depending on their year of birth. Entitlement to the full state pension is dependent on having made NI contributions over at least 90% of your working life.

Is the state pension taxable? Yes, it is. However, there is no mechanism to deduct tax due at source, so those pensioners already on a payroll will have their PAYE code reduced by the amount of the state pension.

9.4.1. Confirm your state pension

As you approach state pension age you should receive a pension enquiry form (P161) from HMRC - it's important that you fill this in in order to make sure you pay the right amount of tax. This form asks for details of your other income and earnings. It will be used to work out the correct PAYE coding for any employment income and second pensions income you might have.

Note. If you're self-employed you won't automatically get Form P161 sent to you. You need to download it or request it from your Tax Office.

9.4.2. State Second Pension (S2P)

In addition to the basic state pension, employees may be credited with additional benefits that have accrued since 1978. This was originally called SERPS (State Earnings Related Pension Scheme) which was reformed into the Second State Pension (S2P) in 2002. This is an earnings-related benefit although the main feature of the S2P is that anyone earning less than a specified minimum will be treated as if they had earnings of that level.

Someone paid at the NI Lower Earnings Level (LEL) (£95 per week for 2009/10) can be put on your business' payroll, have P46 (a form to tell HMRC about an employee who does not have a P45) submitted to HMRC and have their LEL recorded on a P11 deductions working sheet. They will then show up on the Employer's Annual PAYE return to HMRC (P35) at the end of the tax year, receive a P60, and the matching P14 will update their NI record.

They will receive credits for the year which entitle them to a basic state pension and SERPS as if they had earnings of £13,900 for 2009/10.

This is without paying any contributions, as at the LEL they are below the Earnings Threshold at which contributions (employees' plus employers') become payable.

Unfortunately, the self-employed do not qualify for this additional state pension benefit.

TIP

You can obtain a forecast of how much your state pension benefits will be from the Pensions Service by completing Form BR19.

9.4.3. Pension credit

The government has introduced Pension Credit to help those aged 60 or over who have little or no savings at retirement. In 2009/10, for example, if a person or their partner is aged 60 or over, Pension Credit guarantees an income of at least £130.00 per week (single) or £198.45 (couple). It's not taxable. However, as with all state benefits it might be wise not to assume that Pension Credit will be available in future.

9.5. OTHER PENSIONS

Subject to scheme rules, it is possible to take 25% tax-free cash (now called Pension Commencement Lump Sum) from all pension arrangements on your retirement. This lump sum must be taken by age 75, after which time no cash payment of any kind is permitted.

Tax avoidance

Since it is now possible to contribute 100% of earnings into a pension plan and receive full tax relief at your highest rate, there is a clear opportunity at the point of retirement to draw the maximum tax-free lump sum and to reinvest this back into a new pension plan to get tax relief. 25% of this would then be available as tax-free cash, and so the process can be repeated, albeit with ever reducing amounts.

To prevent abuse of this, HMRC have said that they will treat the tax-free amount as an unauthorised payment from your pension fund, which attracts a penalty of at least 40% of the amount paid.

9.6. EMPLOYMENT INCOME

Scenario

Many retired people have multiple employments - two small jobs, or a pension and a job. This puts them at risk of PAYE coding errors.

Example

John retired in May 2009. His employer's pension was modest and he decided to do some part-time work to supplement his income. The money would help make the home more comfortable for him and his wife. He would also be able to keep in touch with the people he had worked with for many years.

What John didn't notice was that he was being given a full personal allowance against his part-time work and the same allowance again, less a deduction for his state pension, against his employer's pension. Over twelve months this would lead to an underpayment of tax of over £1,000.

P46 trap

In these circumstances it is all too easy for an error to be made in the tax code when filling out a Form P46 (a form to tell HMRC about an employee who does not have a P45) when starting work, or by the employer or by HMRC.

Tɪᴘ

Ask for a copy of your P46. It could be worth money if there is an error and you can prove that you did the right thing at the right time. It could reduce the permissible delay by a full twelve months.

Tax avoidance

Tax bills for pensioners caused by HMRC errors can be written off. However, only if you, as the taxpayer, could reasonably have thought your tax was correct. If the tax code was wrong and you did not query it, your request for a write-off will not succeed.

9.7. SELF-EMPLOYMENT

Tax avoidance

If your spouse's pension is not fully utilising their tax-free personal allowance, employ them in your business, and pay them a salary (see Chapter 4) to reduce your taxable profits and use up some more of their personal allowances at the same time.

Tax avoidance

There will nearly always be expenses that are partly business and partly private, such as motoring, Council Tax and fuel bills. You can easily claim a proportion of these as a tax deductible business expense.

Let's say there's a hobby you've always loved. Come early retirement, the hobby blossoms. But when does action figure collecting, selling an Indiana Jones figure to pay for a Luke Skywalker figure, turn from a hobby into a business? How many car boot sales make a trade? When does helping arrange a friend's wedding become something the Tax man is interested in?

Essentially, if you are making or intending to make a profit, you are probably trading. There are various "badges of trade". Online selling is a good example of how you can drift into self-employment.

If you do not register with HMRC, you could be liable to a penalty. In addition there may be penalties of up to 100% of the tax due if you fail to tell HMRC about a new untaxed source of income within six months of the end of the tax year.

9.8. BANK INTEREST

You can apply to your bank to receive interest on your savings without deduction of tax if you expect to have no overall tax liability for the tax year. If you expect to have some liability, even if it is small, you should receive the interest after deduction of tax, but this still leaves you free to apply for a refund from HMRC.

9.9. LETTING OUT A ROOM

Perhaps your home is now a little larger than you need? You may have surplus accommodation and wonder about turning this into cash. The good news is that there is a special tax scheme to help. It is called the "rent-a-room" scheme.

Tax avoidance

Rent-a-room relief enables you to let out a room in your home and exempts the first £4,250 of income from tax. You may provide services, such as meals and laundry as well as charging rent.

9.10. HIRED HELP

After many years of looking after others, do you now need some help yourself? Unfortunately, there are no special tax concessions for those who need personal care in their own homes.

Do you use the services of a gardener, cook or domestic care worker? Perhaps you need someone to help with a few tasks around the house? Maybe you are blind or housebound and have someone help with the shopping or cleaning? In all these cases, you may be surprised to hear that you could be a "micro-employer". And if you are an employer, then you are responsible to deal with the tax.

It is not the amount of money involved, or the number of hours worked that matters here, it is the character of the relationship which counts. Whenever you pay someone for services, particularly where the individual works in your home using your equipment, you need to ask yourself the question "Am I an employer?"

1. Some workers are self-employed. Some of the people who work in homes and provide a variety of help will be self-employed and responsible for their own tax. These individuals may have a number of customers, they may use their own equipment and, most importantly, they may have registered as self-employed with HMRC.

   > **TIP**
   >
   > Ask the individual if they are self-employed. If they are then they should have a unique tax reference number or UTR.

2. Being a micro-employer. If you think you may be a micro-employer, there is some good news for you. HMRC have designed a special Simplified PAYE Deduction Scheme for you - the paperwork may be much easier than you imagined. This scheme is available provided taxable pay is no more than £160 per week, or £700 per month. The scheme can be used if, for example, you employ a nanny, gardener, cook or cleaner. There is more to having an employee than simply tax, so it would be a good idea to take advice. Overall, it makes sense to get the position right now, rather than face questions and possible tax bills later.

9.11. BASIC IHT AVOIDANCE

Recap

Inheritance Tax (IHT) is based on the death value of your estate when it passes to people other than your spouse or a charity. The tax can also be levied on lifetime transfers, either immediately, of if you die within seven years of the transfer. The combined effect of the nil rate band (currently £325,000) and the seven-year cumulative rule can go a long way to mitigating IHT. However, there are gifts and transfers you can make each tax year which will reduce the ultimate tax liability on your estate.

For example, you can give a total of £3,000 without any IHT implications, in addition £5,000 if it is a wedding present to a child, £2,500 to a grandchild getting married or £1,000 to any other person on their marriage. Also, you may give larger sums than all those mentioned above but you would need to survive seven years from the date of the gift for it not to be included in the calculation of your estate.

Tax avoidance

As a couple you each get these limits, so you can give double the amount away in a tax year.

Power of Attorney trap

A Power of Attorney is a legal document allowing, for instance, someone to sign cheques and letters on another's behalf if they were going abroad for some time, became seriously ill or were mentally incapacitated, business and personal interests could be looked after.

The Special Commissioners recently had occasion to consider the validity of IHT gifts made under a Power of Attorney. They decided that the Power of Attorney did not provide expressly, or by implication, for the making of IHT gifts and was therefore void. Accordingly, the deceased had a right to recover the gifts made by his attorneys and that right formed part of the property he was entitled to immediately before his death.

Tax avoidance

Make sure that any Power of Attorney has an express power to cover gifts for IHT purposes. These will keep gifts made by you on their behalf out of their estate and so avoid IHT.

9.12. IHT AND THE FAMILY HOME

Can you give your house to your children to avoid IHT and continue to live in it? Basically, no.

Tax avoidance

To avoid the tax consequences of this, pay a full market rent for living there. However, your children will be taxable on the rent receivable from you.

There are other very complicated schemes around to avoid IHT on the family home but you should consult a tax specialist and a solicitor before embarking on them. Things can get quite complicated but there are genuine opportunities to avoid IHT. Here are a couple of variations which might be relevant to you during this retirement phase of your life.

9.12.1. Scenario one. Living under one roof

Instead of giving your house to your children and continuing to live in it, you and your children could decide to sell your respective houses and buy one huge property for the two families. For illustrative purposes, let us say that the new home will cost £600,000. If property prices revive and then rise at an average of 10% a year, it could be worth £1,170,000 by 2020. If you were to die in 2020, then your estate gets added up to see if there is any IHT to pay.

For example, your estate could be half the house (£585,000), plus savings (say £20,000) and a car (say £10,000), some £615,000 in total. The tax problem being that your family will have to find IHT at 40% of the excess over the tax-exempt so-called nil-rate band (NRB) currently £325,000 and pay this over to the Taxman. At today's rates and thresholds the IHT bill could be £338,000 ((£1,170,000 - £325,000) = £845,000 x 40% IHT rate). So what are your options in avoiding such a large tax bill?

Option 1. Cash gift. One idea would be for you to gift the proceeds from the sale of your property to your children. The children would then buy the new property in their name and you come to live with them. There are two tax problems with this; **(1)** to escape IHT you need to survive the cash gift by seven years; and **(2)** the new pre-owned asset tax (POAT), says you must either pay them market rent for living in the property or suffer an income tax charge levied at 5% p.a. of that market value. Apparently, for the POAT, parents are classed as having given away an asset (the cash) but still enjoying it (i.e. living in a house it was used to buy). Yet another tax catch.

Option 2. Joint owners. As "joint tenants" you all own an equal interest in the whole property. If you both put your respective sale proceeds into the new property and the property is held jointly, when one partner dies the whole of the property automatically passes to the other. This just adds to your own IHT problems, plus you lose any opportunity of saving IHT by passing an interest in the property to the next generation (the grandchildren).

Option 3. Tenants-in-common. The classic IHT saving advice is to pass some of the wealth down a generation to the children on the first (parent's) death, so the surviving parent has a smaller estate to pay IHT on when he or she dies. This is easily done when the family home is held as tenants-in-common, as the deceased's share in the house can be gifted to a younger relative on death leaving the survivor owning half the property but with a right to live in all of it. If the property is held as tenants-in-common (rather than jointly) this allows each party (including you and your spouse) to gift away your share of the property, meaning IHT savings on death.

Download Zone

For free sample **Tenancy-in-common Declaration**, visit **http://books.indicator.co.uk**. You'll find the access code on page 2 of this book.

9.12.2. Scenario two. Funding care home fees

Let's say you are thinking of moving into a care home whose fees will amount to approximately £500 per week. You reckon this can be met out of your savings for a few months, but there will soon be a need to use the substantial capital locked up in your home. The tax problem here is that there is still a potential IHT bill because all you have done is switched your wealth from one asset (property) to another (cash).

Tax avoidance

As an alternative, instead of selling your house, spruce it up and let it out. When you have let property it makes sense to borrow against its capital value, to the extent that the rental income will cover the interest payments due plus necessary repairs and maintenance. This reduces tax you pay on the rental income and releases capital which you can use for any other purpose. You can borrow up to the value of the property on the date it was first made available for letting, with no tax effect. You then can use this released capital to buy an immediate care plan that will pay for the care home fees for the rest of your life.

Note. What is an immediate care plan? This is an assurance product which guarantees to pay a set amount for the individual's remaining life directly to the care home. Once the plan is purchased the capital value is taken out of your estate for IHT.

Tax avoidance

Some years later you die and leave your house to a relative in your will. OK, the value of the house will have increased since you moved into the care home, but after the mortgage has been deducted the net amount might well bring it within the IHT exempt band, so no IHT to pay. And your relative has inherited a valuable asset which already produces an income.

Warning. If you become too ill to sign a Lasting Power of Attorney (LPA), the Office of the Public Guardian will have to appoint a Receiver to handle your financial affairs. The Receiver would not be permitted to let the property and take out the mortgage to release the capital required.

> **Tɪᴘ**
>
> Sign an LPA in someone else's favour now, so that they can handle all your financial affairs, including letting the property, completing tax returns to report the rental income and any other IHT planning moves.

KEY POINTS

Should you be paying tax in retirement?

1. As you approach state pension age you should receive a Pension Enquiry Form P161 from HMRC. Fill it in correctly so that you pay the right amount of tax and get your age-related allowances.

2. HMRC expects everyone to check their own tax code. Many tax codes are incorrect, so this is particularly worth doing.

3. The present structure of the tax system can be very confusing to many people, particularly pensioners. For example, the 10% tax credit on dividends is not repayable, so if your income does not cover your allowances, the dividend credits are wasted.

4. If your income is not fully covered by allowances and deductions, you cannot register to receive bank interest in full, so you may overpay tax and be required to claim a refund.

5. HMRC estimates that there are a large number of pensioners who do not claim the repayments to which they are entitled. Make sure you are not one of them.

6. The marginal tax rate for those over 65 with income over £20,900 can be as high as 33%, so investments that produce tax-free income or capital gains should be considered in those circumstances.

7. In reckoning your income for age allowances, any investment bond withdrawals over the 5% limit have to be taken into account even though there is no tax to pay on the excess at the higher rate. Conversely, the gross amount of a properly recorded donation to a charity reduces your income when calculating whether age allowances are to be restricted. The same applies to personal pension contributions.

8. If your spouse does not have enough income to cover their personal allowance for income tax, you should consider transferring some of your assets to them if practicable, so that the income from them will then be theirs and not yours.

9

Basic IHT avoidance

1. Since lifetime transfers (other than those into trusts) are potentially exempt from IHT and do not have to be reported, it is important to keep accurate records of gifts out of income and capital so there can be no doubt about dates and amounts of gifts.

2. If you make a lifetime gift not covered by the annual exemptions it is essential that the donee is aware that they are responsible for the payment of any IHT on it if you die within seven years.

3. If you become too ill to sign an Lasting Power of Attorney (LPA), the Office of the Public Guardian will have to appoint a Receiver to handle your financial affairs. The Receiver would not be permitted to do things on your behalf, e.g. let the property and take out the mortgage to release the capital required.

CHAPTER 10

Death

10.1. INTRODUCTION

With a house, some savings and perhaps the proceeds of a life assurance policy your estate can easily be worth more than £325,000 - the figure above which Inheritance Tax (IHT) at 40% becomes chargeable for 2009/10. Without the right planning IHT can substantially reduce the value of the estate you leave. In this chapter we've covered several opportunities to mitigate the tax due.

10.2. FIRST STAGE OF IHT AVOIDANCE

Let's say, you are a young professional with a young family, a house, mortgage and no doubt high living expenses. At this stage, your main considerations are likely to be paying off the mortgage, planning for school fees, etc. Here, the IHT avoidance - to the extent that you are concerned about a potential liability that is many years off - should include two elements:

Tax avoidance 1

Put in place an IHT protection policy, written in trust for beneficiaries other than your spouse. This will provide a tax-free sum to help the beneficiaries meet the eventual IHT liability. The monthly/annual premiums are likely to be relatively modest.

Tax avoidance 2

Have a tax effective and flexible will in place which allows for the use of the tax-free threshold for IHT purposes (currently £325,000). This is a relatively inexpensive and simple response to any potential IHT problem. This in turn would require attention to be given to the way in which the estates of you and your partner are held between you.

10.3. YOUR WILL

A will determines exactly who gets what after your death, rather than leaving assets to be divided up according to the intestacy rules. If your estate is likely to be liable to IHT, a tax efficient will is even more important as it could help you save tax or even escape it altogether. What should you include in your will to avoid IHT?

10.3.1. Transfer of spouse's nil-rate band

The nil-rate band (NRB) is currently £325,000 per person, so couples can now protect up to £650,000 of their estate from IHT on the death of the second spouse. This is not a doubling of the tax-free threshold per se, as couples who undertook careful financial planning have always been able to shelter their total tax-free allowance from the Taxman, usually by setting up an NRB trust on the death of the first spouse, but the new rules make this a simpler procedure.

The transferable allowance will be available to all surviving spouses or partners who die on or after October 9 2007, regardless of when the first spouse died. The tax-free threshold available on death of the second spouse will be equivalent to double the NRB applicable at that time.

10.3.2. Have a discretionary will

A discretionary will allows your executors to make decisions according to current tax law, the final assets in the estate and the financial/health circumstances of the surviving spouse and family, following death. However, there is a way you can specify how you would prefer your estate to be distributed.

You will have appointed executors to manage your estate for the benefit of your spouse/family in your will. The executors will have wide powers, not only in relation to the management of the assets of the trust, but also in relation to the timing and manner in which those assets are distributed. However, you can leave them a letter of wishes to follow which includes putting in place a particular IHT planning scheme, e.g. an IOU loan scheme concerning an investment property. As this letter is not legally binding upon the trustees, circumstances may arise under which they consider, quite properly, that to follow it would be inappropriate, i.e. the law changes and the scheme isn't worth implementing.

Apart from major assets, such as a house, there may well be relatively minor items to deal with as part of your estate. Let's say you have made specific bequests of valuable personal items to certain beneficiaries. If you change your mind, you will have the expense of then redrafting clauses in your will. Alternatively, you can draft a letter of wishes outlining what you would like to see happen and lay this alongside your will (but not attached to it).

Tax avoidance

The advantage of this for IHT is that your executors might then be able to include these items in household and personal effects (at one third of insurance value) as part of your estate rather than drawing them to the attention of the Capital Taxes Office (CTO) in the will for separate evaluation for IHT. The CTO does not get to see the letter of wishes, only the will.

10.3.3. Other will points

Spouse inherits all

Since IHT is charged at a single 40% rate on the excess of the estate over the exempt threshold, currently £325,000, no extra IHT savings will be made in transferring an asset from one spouse to another once each has used that nil threshold. It might be better to leave most of the excess over the NRB to the surviving spouse, to avoid tax on the first death and give maximum flexibility for the future.

Not quite all

Since all your gifts to your spouse are exempt from IHT, it is often more tax effective to leave agricultural and/or business property to someone else, otherwise agricultural or business property relief will be wasted. Obviously, the tax position should not override family and other considerations.

Skip a generation

A direct bequest to your grandchildren is better than a bequest to their parent who may have their own IHT problems.

Reviewing wills

Changing legislation, as well as family circumstances, make it important to review wills regularly.

10.4. SECOND STAGE OF IHT AVOIDANCE

IHT is based on the death value of your estate when it passes to people other than your spouse or a charity. The tax may also be levied on lifetime transfers either immediately, or if you die within seven years of the transfer. If you are domiciled in the UK, then your worldwide property will be subject to IHT. If you are not UK domiciled, then only your UK property will be liable.

This is how it might work for you:

ASSETS AND LIABILITIES	£
Value of family home	250,000
Mortgage	(20,000)
Shares	25,000
Building society accounts and ISAs	35,000
Chattels	25,000
Life assurance property claims	60,000
Total	**375,000**
Nil-rate band	325,000
Taxable at 40%	50,000
IHT due	20,000

This second stage is very relevant for high net worth individuals, possibly with children, or a successful entrepreneur considering retirement. At this stage the main priorities are reducing the value of the estate whilst keeping sufficient capital and income to fund an appropriate standard of living. Relevant IHT avoidance includes:

Succession planning

This is crucial for a business whilst preserving any IHT business property relief ("BPR") which is available.

Investing in BPR assets

Consideration could also be given to investing surplus funds in assets which qualify for BPR, commonly known as relievable assets, which are exempt from IHT after two years' ownership, subject to meeting various conditions.

The family home

There are also many ideas involving the family home (see Retirement chapter) which enable the potential taxpayer to remain living in the property while removing a large proportion of the value of the property from their taxable estate. These ideas are too numerous to expand upon here but each situation needs to be assessed in order to advise on the best planning to be used.

In times of low/falling values

Since IHT is less where the value transferred is lower, it's usually beneficial to transfer assets that may grow in value, earlier rather than later. Even if you (the donor) die within seven years, the benefit of transferring assets when their IHT value was lower is retained.

Using trusts

There is also time during this third stage of IHT planning for tax avoidance using trusts.

10.5. BUSINESS PROPERTY RELIEF (BPR)

10.5.1. What qualifies for BPR?

Interests in business and agricultural property may benefit from some extremely valuable reliefs. The reliefs reduce the taxable value for IHT of the transfer by 100% or 50%.

The following qualify for 100% relief:

- the business of a sole trader or interest in a partnership

- shareholdings in an unlisted trading company, including shares in companies listed on the Alternative Investment Market (AIM) and OFEX.

The following qualify for 50% relief:

- shares or securities giving control to a quoted trading company

- land and buildings or machinery or plant, owned by an individual and used wholly or mainly by a trading company under their control, or by a partnership in which they are a partner.

A transfer on death must satisfy several important conditions to qualify for BPR:

- you must have owned the property for at least two years before the date of the transfer

- the relief does not apply to businesses that consist wholly or mainly of dealing in securities, stock or shares, land and buildings, or making or holding investments

- there must be no binding agreement for the sale of the interest in the business

- relief for a trade or trading company shares, can be restricted if any of the assets have not been used mainly for allowable business purposes or are not necessary for future use

- assets received as the original recipient must still own a PET, and they must qualify as business property at the date of death. The relief may still be available if the assets have been replaced with other qualifying assets.

Tax avoidance

The 100% BPR has removed the incentive to make lifetime gifts of the family business. Business assets held at death not only benefit from the effective IHT exemption, but are also passed on to the beneficiary free of CGT (with the exception of some deferred liabilities that become chargeable on death). The value of those assets becomes the beneficiary's base cost for CGT purposes, thus providing a tax-free uplift.

10.6.   TRUSTS AND TAX AVOIDANCE

Many trusts are set up by will as a means of ensuring the desired succession to the deceased's assets. For example, a will might bequeath the income from assets to the deceased's widow and the assets themselves to the deceased's children on the widow's death. The children thereby inherit the assets regardless of the provisions of the widow's will, remarriage of the widow, or the intestacy laws if the widow does not have a valid will.

Lifetime trusts are often used as a means of reducing IHT while avoiding outright gifts in undesirable circumstances, such as where the beneficiaries are children or where the identities of all the eventual beneficiaries are not yet known.

They have also been used to keep landed estates in the family and to protect family property from creditors or from spendthrift family members. Nowadays, almost all lifetime gifts of property into a trust are made in order to gain some form of tax advantage.

TIP

Trusts have many legitimate uses and should be considered in any estate planning exercise. However, there are many circumstances in which tax can arise in connection with the trusts themselves. Care must be taken that you (the settlor) are not merely exchanging one tax liability for another. If you are thinking of entering into any arrangements involving trusts ask in advance about all the risks involved and what fees will be charged; especially for overseas trusts which are often very costly to administer.

10.7. TRUSTS AND IHT PLANNING

10.7.1. Discretionary trust of the nil-rate band

Tax avoidance

A simple tax planning device is to create a discretionary trust with a gift that falls within the donor's IHT nil-rate band. No IHT is payable and the donor can elect to hold over any capital gain. Inheritance tax ten-year and exit charges are likely to be small or nil.

10.7.2. Discretionary trusts in wills

A discretionary trust of the nil-rate band can also be set up in the will of the first to die of a married couple.

Tax avoidance

A reason to use the nil-rate band on first death is that in some circumstances not all the unused nil-rate band can be passed on. This is because the amount of additional nil-rate band that any one surviving spouse or civil partner can accumulate is limited to the value of the nil-rate band in force at the time of their death. This restriction may be relevant where a spouse or partner has had more than one marriage or civil partnership.

10.7.3. Non-tax considerations

For example, you may want to ensure that your children inherit your assets. Passing all assets to a spouse or partner on the first death may not waste a nil-rate band, but if the survivor remarries, the family's wealth may never reach the intended beneficiaries.

Using a discretionary trust preserves flexibility over how the assets will eventually be distributed.

Another use of discretionary trusts in wills is where the testator wants to leave open the precise distribution of assets among beneficiaries. Although wills can be varied, this requires the consent of all beneficiaries affected and is not possible where any of them are minors.

Again, a discretionary trust is more reliable. If the trust lasts for no more than two years, IHT is the same as if the deceased had made the eventual distribution to the beneficiaries.

10.7.4. Non-domiciled settlors

Tax avoidance

Under IHT rules, individuals who are not domiciled in the UK lose that status once they have been resident in the UK for 17 out of the previous 20 tax years. An individual who is about to become UK domiciled can prevent overseas assets from becoming liable to IHT by placing them in a trust.

10.7.5. Passing on the family home

Creating a trust to pass on the family home is normally ineffective for IHT because if the settlor continues to live in the home rent-free, they have retained a benefit. Schemes involving trusts were devised to try to get around this problem, with varying degrees of success.

10.7.6. Pre-owned assets tax (POAT)

Income tax (POAT) is charged on the benefit people get by having free or low-cost enjoyment or use of certain assets they formerly owned, or provided the funds to purchase. It applies to all arrangements set up from March 18 1986 onwards if the former owner of an asset still enjoys a benefit, with some limited exceptions.

Example

In January 2009, Ian gifted shares worth around £70,000 in Owzatt Management Ltd to his son Alan. In May 2009 these shares were sold for some £100,000. His son used the proceeds towards the purchase of a bungalow for £150,000 which was occupied by Ian as his main residence on a rent-free basis. The annual rental value of the bungalow in 2009/10 onwards is £16,000.

In this case the shares are "other property" under pre-owned asset rules that were sold by Alan with the proceeds being used to buy an interest in land (the bungalow) to be occupied by his father.

Ian will have an annual POAT value of £10,667. This is calculated as £16,000 x (£100,000/£150,000) = £10,667.

The income tax charge pre-owned assets is not limited to arrangements involving property or even arrangements involving trusts, but also extends to chattels (tangible movable assets, such as works of art) and financial products. If you benefit from having free or low cost enjoyment of chattels (such as valuable paintings or ornaments) that you formerly owned. The calculation of the POAT charge for chattels is slightly different in that the official rate of interest (currently 4.75%) is applied.

Tax avoidance

There is no POA charge if your total taxable amount for the tax year does not exceed £5,000. However, this is not an exempt band so that an annual rental value of, say, £5,100 would be fully chargeable to POA tax.

Tax avoidance

If past IHT planning has resulted in liability to income tax on pre-owned assets, it might be possible to save money by paying something for the "benefit" received. For example, a person who continues to live in property given away could pay rent. This is a complicated area and specialist advice should be obtained.

10.7.7. Insurance and pensions

It is possible to enter into an insurance policy that will pay out a lump sum on death that can be used to pay IHT. Such policies should be written in trust so that the payout falls out of the estate. Premiums paid would normally be covered by the IHT annual and normal expenditure from income exemptions. The same is true for death benefits under pension schemes, which are exempt from the changes in the **Finance Act 2006**.

10.8.   DEATHBED PLANNING

At death the value of the estate, together with the value of all lifetime gifts, but not exempt gifts, made in the proceeding seven years is calculated and the appropriate amount of tax is charged.

The third stage of IHT avoidance is often referred to as deathbed planning. This is where the individual may not have long to live and no tax planning has been put in place so most common forms of planning (e.g. surviving a gift by seven years) are inappropriate.

10.8.1. Make a will

Even with deathbed situations a tax effective and flexible will can help you avoid IHT.

10.8.2. Use those annual exemptions

Tax avoidance

There are still lots of gifts and transfers you can make each year as part of deathbed planning , which enable you to avoid IHT altogether. These include:

- **£3,000.** Each individual may give £3,000 away every year without any IHT consequence at all. If you did not use this last year, then you may carry it forward and give away £6,000 this year. So a husband and wife can give £12,000 away, thus saving £4,800 (£12,000 x 40%) in potential tax.

- **£250 gifts.** Gifts of up to £250 may be given to anybody.

- **Normal expenditure out of income.** You can give away almost any amount as long as it is seen to be normal expenditure from your income, is not manifestly from capital, and is capable of being repeated year on year.

10.8.3. Take a spouse or civil partner

Tax avoidance

Leaving everything to your spouse would exempt your whole estate from IHT. Whereas as a single person you are liable to IHT at 40% on the value of your estate over £325,000. If your estate exceeds this amount during your deathbed planning phase, consider taking on a spouse just to save IHT.

10.8.4. Records

TIP

It will make your executors' task far easier if you keep an up-to-date schedule of your investments, mortgages, pensions, etc. with your will showing where all the relevant documents are kept. Any potentially exempt gifts for IHT should also be recorded.

10.9. POST-DEATH PLANNING

The final stage of IHT avoidance - and this may surprise you - is post-death planning.

10.9.1. Deeds of Variation

The tax planning idea here is a Deed of Variation (DoV), which can be used if the deceased's will was not as tax effective or as flexible as it could have been or the person died intestate. It can be used to make sure that the available tax-free threshold can still be utilised.

The effect of the DoV is to allow the estate to be distributed tax effectively with the new gifts being treated for IHT purposes as if they were made by the deceased in their will. The DoV must be put in place within two years of death and be agreed to by the beneficiaries affected. This can be a good way of diverting wealth to children where beneficiaries are already wealthy in their own right and do not want to exacerbate their own potential future IHT problem.

> TIP
>
> Although, if they all agree, those entitled to your estate have the right to vary the way it is to be distributed, it is sometimes useful for your will to contain authority for a DoV, since this may help your beneficiaries to understand that they wouldn't be acting against your wishes.

10.9.2. Fall in asset values

For CGT purposes, those entitled to assets in a deceased's estate acquire them at market value at the date of death. If assets have fallen since death, the beneficiaries cannot use losses made by the personal representatives on disposal.

10.9.3. Paying the tax

Although winding up an estate can take a long time, IHT is payable six months after death. As a result it is often necessary to make payments to HMRC on account, to avoid building up interest charges. The personal representatives might have to borrow the money, because it might not be possible to realise cash from the estate quickly enough.

Tax on some assets can be paid by instalments over ten years. These assets include: land and buildings; a controlling shareholding in a company; some shareholdings in unquoted companies; an interest in an unincorporated business.

For shares and securities giving control, and for land and buildings included in a business or partnership, interest is payable in instalments only when these are not paid on time. For other assets, interest is charged on the full amount outstanding at the rate in force at the time.

Administering a deceased's estate and accounting for IHT on that gets complicated, and this section is for general tax saving advice only. So for specific problems and individual planning, it is essential to obtain competent professional advice tailored to individual needs.

KEY POINTS

Basic IHT planning

1. Put in place an insurance policy, written in trust. Increase the sum assured to provide a tax-free sum to help your beneficiaries meet any IHT liability. The monthly/annual premiums for this can also reduce your estate for IHT purposes.

2. Have in place a tax effective and flexible will which allows for the use of the tax-free threshold for IHT purposes (currently £325,000).

3. You can give away almost any amount as long as it is seen to be normal expenditure from your income, is not manifestly from capital, and is capable of being repeated year on year.

Wills

1. Leaving everything to your spouse in your will would exempt your entire estate from IHT.

2. Since all gifts to your spouse are exempt from IHT, it is often more tax effective to leave agricultural and/or business property to someone else, otherwise agricultural or business property relief will be wasted.

3. A direct bequest to your grandchildren is better than a bequest to their parent who may have their own IHT problems.

4. In your will you will have appointed executors to manage your estate for the benefit of your spouse/family. Leave them a letter of wishes to follow which includes putting in place a particular IHT planning scheme. As this letter is not legally binding upon the trustees, circumstances may arise under which they consider, quite properly, that to follow it would be inappropriate.

Business property relief (BPR)

1. Business assets held at death can qualify for an effective 100% or 50% IHT exemption. BPR may be restricted or lost for non-business use of assets or resources. Preserving BPR is therefore an important part of tax avoidance.

2. Secured loans are deducted from the value of the asset on which they are secured. So, normally a mortgage secured on business property that qualifies for relief should, where feasible, be transferred to a residential property. This reduces the taxable estate and could therefore save many thousands of pounds in IHT.

Pre-owned Assets (POAT)

1. POAT is charged on the benefit people get by having free or low-cost enjoyment or use of certain assets they formerly owned, or provided the funds to purchase.

2. If past IHT planning has resulted in liability to POAT, it might be possible to save money by paying something for the "benefit" received. For example, a person who continues to live in property given away could pay rent.

3. There is no POA charge if your total taxable amount for the tax year does not exceed £5,000. However, this is not an exempt band so that an annual rental value of, say £5,100 would be fully chargeable to POA tax.

Post-death planning

1. You can use a Deed of Variation (DOV) if the deceased's will was not as tax effective nor flexible as it could have been or the person died intestate.

2. For Capital Gains Tax purposes, those entitled to assets in a deceased's estate acquire them at market value at the date of death. If asset values are falling post-death, then transfer the assets themselves, rather than the cash proceeds from their sale, to the beneficiaries. Any loss on disposal then becomes tax deductible for the beneficiary.